Learning From Jane

Touched by God, a Witness of Great Faith and Courage

By Calvin L. Keeler, Sr.

TATE PUBLISHING, LLC

Dedication

To Jane, who loved and adored me so much, who made my life better every day, who was a most wonderful wife and partner, and who taught me so much about life and sharing.

Table of Contents

Foreword. 9

Chapter 1 - Beginnings 1932 - 1947. 17

Chapter 2 - The Early Years 1948 - 1953 27

Chapter 3 - Just Married 1953 - 1954. 41

Chapter 4 - Illness Begins 1954 - 1955. 55

Chapter 5 - Living is Wonderful 1955 - 1960. . . 71

Chapter 6 - Making the Most of It 1960 - 1970 . 83

Chapter 7 - The Good Years 1971 - 1986 98

Chapter 8 - Succeeding in the Struggle with Illness
    1987–1998 115

Chapter 9 - Triumph in the Final Years
    1999 - 2002. 137

Chapter 10 - After 171

Chapter 11 - The Lessons Of Life. 181

Appendix A - Order of Funeral Service 197

Appendix B - Husband's Words for Jane Wiley
    Keeler at the Funeral Service 201

Appendix C - Words of Condolence Received by Email and by Card 215

Appendix D - Excerpts from Delaware Physician's Letters. 220

Appendix E - Several of Jane's Favorite Recipes. 223

Foreword

This is the story of triumphant living in spite of an overwhelming life-long illness and of two people devoted to each other through good times and bad times. It is a story of true love growing progressively stronger and deeper every year. Moreover, it is the story of the touch of God on the lives of two people who were committed to the Christian faith and who shared a firm belief in Him. The life of my wife is evidence of the power of prayer and is demonstrable proof that God's miracles are still bestowed upon us in modern times in the real world.

This is the story of how my wife, Jane, progressively learned her lessons of this life, while enduring a lifetime of severe illness. We do not know all of our lessons when we are young, some are learned early, many are learned in the last months of life, and some are never learned, but learning is what we do to prepare ourselves to fulfill our purpose. Learning is a life-long process. The most important lesson was that she learned to share in the love and energy of our creator and the source of our life, God.

Jane was never famous, was not in the government, was not a leader in industry, and was not a leading scholar. However, she understood the meaning of life, and she was a witness to God's power and love, as she touched the lives of many who met her. We did not believe that life is just a test to determine if we are good or evil on judgment day. Rather life is an opportunity to experience and enjoy a wonderful world and an opportunity to learn how to live, to learn about God's love, to learn how to share in that love, and then to teach others to share in that love.

She was subjected to over seventy hospital admissions, over twenty major surgeries of three to eight hours duration each, and in her final two years of life was sedated in intensive care units for over six months. None of this changed her resolve to live a full life upon every hospital discharge with as much normalcy as possible.

During the latter years of my wife's life, I watched Jane struggle to live and to make a statement with her life. She exhibited tremendous bravery and courage with no fear of death and demonstrated a full acceptance that she would pass to be in God's presence. She was an energetic and active person, and had extraordinary will power. She had an unshakeable faith and was determined to live a full and normal life, no matter what might be the obstacles, and to overcome every trial and test.

She never objected to being admitted to a hospital because she had complete faith that every time they would assist her healing and send her home better. While she was in the hospital, she always kept the clear goal and vision and real expectation of being discharged much better. Researchers have recently learned how important it is for everyone to visualize a desired outcome. She never feared surgery, but just put her life in the hands of God, her surgeons, and her medical team. Hers was an heroic struggle against unrelenting disease. I have never ceased to be amazed at her strong faith, her acceptance of her condition without anger or stress, her unending struggle to live a normal life, her deepening faith as her life waned, and putting all in the hands of God.

There were two principles that she repeatedly demonstrated to those with whom she came in contact. First, her faith in God was deep and unshakeable, and it was present in her every action. Secondly, life is a wonderful gift to be enjoyed and valued for as long as possible. She was grateful for each new day and lived a life of thankfulness.

After all of the struggles in the latter years of her life had ended and I had time to reflect about them all, I realized that I needed to write a book about her life and her journey. Her journey was awesome, and needs to be remembered. If one did not look closely, some of the subtleties of her life might be missed. As I thought about what I would write, I realized that both her life and my life were so intertwined that I would need to write about us together. Therefore, part of what I write will be biographical and part will be autobiographical, but only as necessary to report on her life.

Her impact on my life has been deeper and more overwhelming than anything I had realized up until I took the time to consider her contributions as a whole. In retrospect, I have come to realize the progression in her journey, and how deeply she touched those about her both in Massachusetts and in Delaware. People whom she met have been inspired by her faith, strength, and courage. Years later, they remind me of how their paths had crossed, and I would like to report that story.

This is a life-long process or journey. I will not list all of the inspiring events, nor will I itemize or dwell on the mistakes that we both made over the years. Neither one of us was perfect, for we were and are imperfect human beings. We each made our share of mistakes (many of my own are very clear to me), and there are choices which we wish that we could have changed. There are many lessons that we each should have learned, but did not. Learning lessons is a progressive experience throughout life with some lessons learned early and some much later. Further, each of us in this life has our own distinctive lessons to learn, with more or less success. There will be no attempt here to itemize or categorize all of the lessons that one might learn in this life. I will instead report on the process for us, which, I hope, can be instructive and suggestive to others.

I learned much from Jane. She taught me to be practical and how to live in this world, since I had spent so many of my early years and energy in formal education. She taught me to enjoy living. She showed and taught me much about true love. And, of course, she taught me about patience, about persistence, and about never quitting.

Throughout my life, I have been guided by ideas and thoughts that have come to me during my quiet moments of meditation and prayer. I have always believed that these have come directly from

                                    Calvin Keeler, Sr.

God to help me in my life. This guidance has assisted my spiritual life, as well as my work life and my home life. It has helped add meaning to each event in my life.

In the months since my wife's death, her purpose and meaning in life have become clearer to me each day, and I feel obliged to share our experience. As her journey neared its end, the lessons that she had learned became more apparent, just as her faith and closeness to God became more profound.

From the thousands of precious moments, events, medical procedures, good times, and bad times of our lives, I have tried to select those that are the most meaningful for this book. Every day, I remember another forgotten doctor's visit, another hospitalization, or another test that she endured gracefully. As you read, I urge you to not forget that each of us believed that we shared a wonderful life and that we lived in the best of times with tremendous happiness. We believed that we had the opportunity to experience much of God's great creation and enjoyed the beauty of it every day. We felt touched by God. We did almost everything in this life for which we ever wished. Neither of us ever felt incomplete or cheated in any way. There were no unmet adventures. We did not feel "if only-." We actually found daily happiness and enjoyment, benefited from daily challenges and experiences, and together with our son had some wonderful quiet times and vacations.

There is no way that I can fully express my appreciation and thanks to my dear wife, Jane, for sharing her life and journey with me. I thank her for a wonderful life, made more meaningful each day both by her love and total devotion to me and by her understanding of the lessons of life. I feel very blessed and fortunate to have lived my life with Jane. She taught me many lessons that I could not have learned anywhere else. She was the best person I have ever met, and I was honored by her presence. I cannot but wonder why I was so fortunate.

I wish to thank my parents, Rev. Herman and Gladys Keeler, for loving me and for establishing me in The Faith before my earliest recollections and while still in their arms, and then their working tirelessly for me to mature in life and in faith, and to be my own person. They put my well-being before their own.

I wish to thank Jane's parents, Ambrose and Georgia Wiley, for nurturing and developing their daughter so well and for supporting and instilling an appreciation and commitment to the Christian gospel and way of life. She absorbed marvelous standards and morals.

For his contributions in helping write this book I wish to thank my son, Dr. Calvin L. Keeler, Jr., who supported and stood my his mother and me for the entire journey. I also wish to thank Dr. Sharon Keeler, my son's wife, along with our son for the many important suggestions and large effort they expended in assisting the editing of this manuscript.

I wish to thank Rev. Susan Morrison, our pastor at the Lexington United Methodist Church,

Calvin Keeler, Sr.

who visited Jane very faithfully from 1995 until her final visits to the Massachusetts General Hospital in 2000, and even after we had moved to our home in Delaware, and who also supported me in my writing of this book.

I wish especially to thank Marilyn Wise (social worker at the Massachusetts General Hospital) for urging me to complete this work and for her many hours and days spent editing and making very insightful and critical suggestions for this manuscript.

I wish to thank all of the many physicians, and especially many exceptional ones whose names are referenced in the book, who expended such effort to give Jane the opportunity to live her life the way she wanted to live it: primary physicians, surgeons, endocrinologists, infectious disease specialists, gastroenterologists, nephrologists, critical care specialists, ophthmalogists, neurosurgeons, orthopedicians, pain clinicians, and many others. I wish also to thank the medical teams in the hospitals, the laboratories, and the visiting nurse associations for their devoted care. Moreover, I wish to thank the hospitals: the Massachusetts General Hospital, the Mount Auburn Hospital, and the Boston Lying In Hospital in Massachusetts, and the Christiana Hospital in Delaware for their enlightened and thoughtful care and support.

Chapter 1

Beginnings

1932 - 1948

This is an account of how Jane, while in this human life, grew and developed day by day. With a strong and deep faith, my wife learned lessons that we are meant to learn in this existence, both in her living and in her soul, so that in the end she was ready to move to a higher plane of existence in the next life. I believe that how well we listen and learn determines both this life and the next life.

My wife was born on a cold winter night just before midnight on February 19, 1932, in Calais, Maine, very close to the Canadian border. She and her mother shared the same birthday and always enjoyed celebrating together on those days for as long as her mother was alive.

Jane's father was Ambrose E. Wiley, and her mother's maiden name was Georgia Campbell. They were married in 1922, and together they raised a family of five children, teaching them right from wrong.

They were hard working, God-fearing, and went to church every Sunday. Jane's father held several different jobs throughout his life from a bookkeeper in the logging country in Maine to a machinist in Connecticut, and later as a minister to a small church in New Hampshire. Jane's mother took care of the family at home, but after the children were grown, helped with several jobs in the manufacturing sector from time to time. They both worked very hard to provide a good and honorable life for their children.

Jane had three older sisters: Lois, Eileen, and Winifred, who grew up and played together. Jane was the fourth child, with three years separating Jane from her next older sister. There also was a younger brother, Douglas, born two years after Jane. The family lived across the street from a Reformed Baptist Church, which they attended several times a week. In addition, when there were guest ministers, the family often enjoyed providing Sunday dinner for the visitors. I have been told that some members of the church would gather for singing and a hoe-down with accordion playing by the Wiley family on Saturday nights. That is how well my wife participated in growing up in the faith at such an early age.

As an example, while still a young girl, and before elementary school years, she and her brother would hold Sunday school in the shed in back of the house and urge their other young pals and friends in the neighborhood to attend this unusual Sunday school. Jane also learned to play the accordion, but never played it in my presence.

She had many happy memories while growing up and fondly remembered when she was three to four years old that after supper she would sit on her father's lap in the living room and listen to the evening news on the radio. When Jane was still young, her father challenged her on one New Year's Day to learn the scripture verses on the calendar for a whole year. Religious calendars in that period had a different scripture verse for each of the 365 days. At the end of the year, she recited each day's scripture reference and verse for the entire year in order. She missed one day from the last week of the year. This was an excellent accomplishment, but she was told that she was not successful. In retrospect and fortunately for Jane, this was a harsh, but valuable and tough lesson, learned very early in life. For all of her life she believed that if anything was worth doing, it was worth doing absolutely correctly and as well as you could, be it schooling, study, prayer, trying to get well from sickness, working, cooking, cleaning, recreation, or entertaining. This was actually a vital and necessary lesson to prepare her for the hard life she would be required to endure with such a strong spirit in her later days. The proof of her discipline would be demonstrated later in junior high school, high school, college, and adult life. Would that we all had learned such a hard lesson.

She recounted many good memories of her childhood: of visiting a large extended family, of visiting an aunt and uncle on the farm and feeding the animals, of crossing the bridge into Canada to go shopping, of sliding in the Maine snows, of porch swings, of church attendance, of boating on a lake with other family members, and of camp meetings in Canada. She played mostly with her younger brother during the early years, but as she grew to maturity, she became ever closer to her three older sisters.

Her birth certificate was written as "Mary Jane Wiley." At an early age, Jane took it upon herself to modify her name, and this is an example of how she shaped her own persona. When she entered first grade, she was enrolled with the name "Mary Jane." She did not object to being called "Mary Jane" or "Jane," but did not want to be called "Mary," which was what everyone began to call her. Thus, she told her teacher and her school chums right away that her name instead was "Jane Mary Wiley." Later when the first communication from the teacher came home, her mother asked about the name change. Jane explained what she had done and why, and that ended the discussion. For the rest of her life, she was known as "Jane." In later years, we named our sailboat "Mary Jane" in her honor. She really enjoyed that and thought that it was nifty.

When she entered first grade in 1937, she was left-handed. At that period in the public school system, it was believed that a child should be taught to be right-handed. After much intervention, Jane became ambidextrous and could use either hand for almost any task. In later life, she did use her right hand for writing. However, her hand dexterity was

Calvin Keeler, Sr.

excellent for both hands, and she used them almost interchangeably for most tasks.

On December 7, 1941, Japan attacked the United States at Pearl Harbor and the Second World War began. In 1942, in order to find better work with higher pay, the entire family of two parents and five children moved to Hartford, Connecticut. Her father found work at the Pratt & Whitney Aircraft Co., the local aircraft engine plant. Work had been very difficult to find in Maine in the years just preceding this. In Hartford, they began to attend the church where my father was the minister. Strangely, this church was a different Protestant denomination from the one which they had been attending in Maine. I remember nothing of these days concerning Jane. At the close of the war in 1945, the two parents, along with Jane and her younger brother moved back to Calais, Maine, while the three older sisters remained in Hartford, since they had found permanent work and liked the city.

Jane returned to school in Calais for the next year in the ninth grade. During this time, the family continued its emphasis on religion, and Jane vividly recalled attending a camp meeting at the Saint John River near St. John, New Brunswick, Canada during her early teenage years. She remained friends for years with the camp counselors and remembered the singing, praying, and her own baptism in the river. She also vividly remembered the drowning of a close friend while he was swimming in the river.

Since her hometown of Calais was across

the river from the city of Saint Stephen, Canada, Jane crossed the bridge almost daily to shop in Saint Stephen, where there were more and better stores. She appeared to have had a typical conservative and religious upbringing in a small town.

She took a required class in cooking when she was in junior high school. The girls in the class invited their mothers in for a meal so that they could demonstrate their cooking skills. The other girls were unable to make white sauce, which was needed in the cooking recipes. Only Jane could make it, and so she did. Her mother had never given her formal cooking lessons, but Jane must have observed and learned more about cooking over the early years that what she had realized. For all of her life, Jane was a natural cook who could cook anything and was not afraid to try and even modify recipes on the fly.

Jane was an extraordinary person. In grade school, her teachers had suggested that students should learn two words from the dictionary every night. Jane is the only person I know who ever did this. I certainly did not. Thus in later years Jane's vocabulary was impressive. During high school, she also wanted to learn as much culture as she could, and so she read many portions of Emily Post's "Book of Etiquette." She also took an active interest in listening to opera and classical music, both orchestra and piano. There was no way that she could have known how essential these skills that she was acquiring would be to her in her later life.

In addition to the coincidence of Jane's fam-

     Calvin Keeler, Sr.

ily moving to Hartford and of attending the same church that I attended, three more events occurred which seem as though "they were supposed to be." Most people believe that there are "coincidences" at major turning points in our lives. However, to me a more plausible explanation is that some things are just supposed to happen. These are possibilities, opportunities, and gifts granted to us by our creator, our God, if we are open to His guidance. God has given us free will and choices in our lives with alternatives, but if we follow the right paths and accept guidance, certain beneficial results appear to follow. However, due to our free will and the exercise of our freedom of choice, things that are "supposed to be" do not "have to be." We believe that it is up to us as individuals to choose our own way, since the world is not fixed and predetermined, but rather has freedom of choice. We believe that these events should not be called "luck."

The first additional example is that in the ninth grade in Calais and later in Bulkeley High School in Hartford, Connecticut, for the 10th through 12th grades, Jane wanted to prepare for college and to take the appropriate courses. However, her family and school officials urged her to take commercial courses so that she would be prepared to get a typical job for a young girl when she graduated from high school. She only knew that she wanted to be a professional person. She had no way of knowing how important a decision this would be to her future in finding me and to our life together. I do not know how, but she negotiated with each of these school systems by herself and finally reached a compromise by taking some pre-college courses along with all the commercial courses. This required obtaining personal approval from the principals and a lot of extra work for her. The result was that upon graduation from high school, she was a very highly skilled secretary and also prepared to begin college work, both of which she did soon thereafter.

A second coincidence was that in 1946 the family moved to Hartford, Connecticut for a second time because of the continuing scarcity of job opportunities in the area of Calais, Maine.

The third coincidence occurred because at this time, there arose a misunderstanding between the Wiley family and my father, the minister of the church, which resulted in Jane's mother and father attending a different church in Hartford. For some reason, Jane decided that she wished to continue to attend the church where my father was the minister. It was not to be near me, since we did not know each other. Her family strenuously attempted to persuade her to go to their new church, but she refused, even though it meant at least twice a week she would need to take a bus by herself from church to her home in a different part of the city late at night.

The strength of her convictions, when she felt guided, was always strong throughout her life. If any of these items had not occurred, then I very much doubt that we would have dated and gotten to know

                                            Calvin Keeler, Sr.

each other. I also believe that each of our lives would have been very different and much less complete.

It is clear from Jane's actions and from her later conversations with me that by this time she had developed a dream, or a set of goals for herself.

• As she told me later and near the end, she wanted to "be a good girl," which meant that she wanted to live a Christian life, following all of the teachings of the Bible. She wanted to be an old fashioned girl but be fully adept at all the modern technologies.

• She wanted to be a professional person and get a good college education.

• She wanted to marry a professional Christian man.

• She wanted a quiet, sedate, well decorated and furnished home in a good part of town.

• She wanted to cook and clean and have a distinctive home.

• She wanted to be a devout Christian and attend church regularly.

• She wanted a family of six boys (she was very happy with the one boy that she had, and he made up for all of the others).

Of course, this dream grew and changed during her life as Jane learned more and more lessons. But, what a wonderful start for a young person to have such dreams!

Chapter 2

The Early Years

1948 - 1953

In August in the summer of 1948, I called Jane and requested a date to go to a minor league baseball game in Hartford, Connecticut. This was one of those things that was meant to be. During my early years I had had only a very few dates, since I did not have a great interest in dating girls. Having just graduated from high school in June of 1948, I was wondering if there were any girls from my church that I might ask out on a date. Jane was a year and one-half younger than I, and a class behind. She was sixteen, and I was just a few days past my eighteenth birthday. About all I knew of her was her name. There was no clear reason for me to call her, although she and my sister were quite friendly.

As she told me later, she really hated base-ball, but that she wanted to go out with me. I do not recall much about the baseball game except that we arrived late (my fault, as usual). Years later she told me that after the first date she was very interested in me and that she wanted to date only me from then on. She decided to go "steady." Although I did not date any other girls, it took me over two years to commit myself to being "steady." It took me until some time later to understand the very close attachment that we were developing.

As I was just entering college in 1948, we got together only a few times during that year. I remember giving her a large box of chocolates for Christmas. In the next year, Jane graduated from high school in June of 1949. Due to the differences over church issues between my father and her family and their attending a different church, my parents were trying to break us up and suggested that I do something else out of town with them on her graduation night. Thus, I did not attend her high school graduation. To her surprise, at her graduation, she won a prize in English. I have regretted ever since not attending this important event for her.

Jane and I dated from 1948 until we married in January 1953. For the first three years I was still attending college and unsure of my own directions. Since I completed four full years of college work in three years, it required fully dedicating myself to my college work. My life was made easier because she understood so much so early in our relationship and was not demanding, but just stood by and waited. Being immersed in college work, during the first two years the number and timing of dates were erratic, except that we usually saw each other at church

                                    Calvin Keeler, Sr.

and on Sunday afternoons. I was even not available much in the summers, since I was busy in my college studies. Dates were occasional and irregular. Nevertheless, we each remained true to the other.

I had lived a very sheltered life. One day in 1950, Jane invited me to go to a pizza restaurant on a side street in downtown Hartford. At the age of 20, I did not know what a pizza was, and I felt like I was going to a place of wickedness. I survived and have enjoyed pizzas ever since. Jane was no less sheltered in her own way. In my freshman year at college, I was on the third or fourth string for freshman soccer when she came to watch me at a game. I was such a poor player that I think that my only job on that day was to run the sidelines to flag out of bounds on the ball. She told me later that she was somewhat embarrassed to see me in my soccer uniform shorts. I guess neither of us was yet prepared for the big real world.

By 1951, in our third year, our dating became more regular, and we attended many organ recitals throughout the Hartford area. One of my close college friends was an outstanding organist, and I frequently turned music pages for his practices and occasionally turned pages for his recitals. At times, several organists who had a worldwide reputation gave some recitals in the city, which Jane and I attended. During this third year we began to take short drives around the area at least once a week, just to be alone together and to talk.

I remember a large number of our dates were spent discussing philosophy, religion, history, and literature. Jane and I spent much of our time together enjoying a good conversation about these important issues. I remember our conversations about the plays of Shakespeare (she really liked Shakespeare and other good literature), about church, and about religion. I especially remember our discussions concerning an idea from the ancient Greek philosophers that every so often two people are fortunate in finding the other half to their own soul. Jane and I felt very strongly that we each found the other half of our souls in the other, making one complete soul. This is a much deeper concept than the current common language of "soul mates" and is truly rare. Later in life, it appeared many times as though we shared a single consciousness.

Throughout our life together, I do not remember any substantive disagreements on any fundamental or major issues. Of course, there were disagreements and sometimes angry words, but they were minor and primarily tactical about daily issues. These problems rarely lasted more than one day.

It was about this time in our third year of dating that I began to discover a truly deep attachment for Jane. I, too, now felt that we were going steady. I began to understand love for another person during this period, reciprocating her love for me since our very first date. Engagement for marriage and that next level of commitment to each other did not occur until early 1953, in our fifth year of dating.

We enjoyed taking afternoon rides on the weekends and finding a quiet spot with a beautiful

 Calvin Keeler, Sr.

view of trees, fields, and hills, where we could have our discussions. Several times over the years, we took day trips by car over the Mohawk trail in western Massachusetts to view the beautiful fall foliage in the mountains.

Before we were engaged, Jane's friends at work began to suggest that I was "stringing her along" and that I would never make a commitment to marry her. They suggested that she find another person to date. However, she never wavered.

During this time of our five-year courtship, we both went to the same church and also held similar conservative views on religion. Typically on each Sunday for all fifty-two weeks of the year, we attended Sunday school and three worship services, one of which was a little less formal. We also each attended a prayer service in the middle of the week, and by the fifth year, we were each attending a second prayer service on Saturday night. We learned to pray, to listen to God, to sing in choirs, and to meditate. Jane loved to sing the old gospel hymns, and she also enjoyed listening to recordings of the old country gospel hymns. This formative training and grounding instilled values, which were essential for the struggles that life presented to us later.

Without this personal commitment of both of our lives to our faith and without our absorbing the gospel in our souls and in our motivations, I doubt that either of us would have had the courage and strength to endure the hard road ahead of us. We always felt that we were a small part of something much grander and eternal.

During the latter two years of our courtship, I was attending graduate school and earning my Master of Arts degree in mathematics at Harvard University in Cambridge, Massachusetts. I enjoyed her frequent telephone calls and almost daily letters. We still saw a good deal of each other, since I traveled home to her, to my family, and to my church each weekend. It was about a two-hour trip by bus each way. Several times Jane traveled to Cambridge and visited. We enjoyed watching several live professional performances of Shakespearean plays at the Cambridge Brattle Theater and attended several organ concerts. We truly enjoyed talking to each other, and we truly enjoyed just being in each other's company. We grew much closer during my first year at graduate school and became engaged during my second year.

We believed that marriage should be based upon a respect for each other and upon a compatibility of the spirit or soul. We also believed that physical attraction was not the only basis for marriage, and therefore we were abstinent and waited until married. The modern concepts of "consenting adults" and "no harm done" are just not valid as a basis for a true and lasting relationship. It does do harm—the relationship of souls is subverted by the physical. Marriage that is based upon a physical attraction and attachment must be improved over the years into the true relationship of marriage for it to survive, if it can. It must be redeemed. Since in our culture it frequently does not survive, then it appears that this change is difficult to accomplish for those who get things in the wrong order.

Modern culture suggests that young people should find someone with whom they can be "happy." Unfortunately, the search for happiness does not usually find happiness. The correct approach is not to search for happiness by itself, but to search for someone to share one's life and love with, to search for someone who has similar visions and interests, that is at least a soul mate. Then happiness will usually follow.

During our courtship, Jane was able to grow her own personal life with her own will power. After graduation in June of 1949, Jane began work at the probate court in Hartford. She had become an outstanding secretary and impressed the judge with the speed and accuracy of her dictation and typing. As you may remember, there were no tape recorders or computers in 1949, and a secretary took dictation in shorthand and later transcribed it on a mechanical typewriter (electric models were too slow in the late 1940's). Being in court work, each page had to be absolutely error-free with no corrections or erasures. Jane worked at the court for two years and became a favorite of the judge, who took her for transcripts on hearings at institutions around the state wherever they were held.

She excelled and had learned her secretarial course skills in high school very well. She stood out in an office of more than a dozen secretaries. She demanded very high standards of performance for herself and had the dedication and commitment to get the work done very fast and correctly. She used to test and time her dictating rate and typing speeds and accepted the challenge of being the fastest that she could. She had been a close second to top honors upon high school graduation for her speed of dictation and typing.

She had many friends in high school and in her early jobs, as she was popular. In high school, she became a little less popular when she decided not to join a sorority. In her early jobs, she enjoyed her lunches out and shopping trips with the girls. She did not realize how popular she was in church until she was urged to let her name be put up for president of the young people's group against a very popular young fellow. Along with the leaders of the church, she could not believe it when she won the election. She performed her tasks as president of the group very well.

The judge was an important person in Hartford, and as an example of his concern for Jane, he inquired of his associates and contacts that he knew at my college to determine if I would be a worthy suitor. It appears that he approved our courtship.

Every Christmas, our church put on a big pageant, which involved every child in the Sunday school. In preparation for this event, Jane was accustomed for several years to spending several evenings at my house, the parsonage, typing the script with carbon copies for the event.

   Calvin Keeler, Sr.

In order to raise her level of income, Jane next worked as a private senior secretary at a manufacturer's association where she became involved in trade, tariffs, and transportation projects. Her manager was very supportive and encouraging, and assigned her more and more work and responsibility along with more complexity. Her manager continually and intentionally challenged her by dictating faster and faster and making the words more complex. She accepted the challenge and exceeded. Her manager was accustomed to taking her to hearings regarding tariff issues so that she could provide transcripts. At one such meeting, the president of a company asked if she might be interested in dating his son. She replied that she was already committed. Again, she did very well and remained at this position until we were married in 1953 and she moved with me to Cambridge, Massachusetts.

During this period of working for four years, she learned to act and dress professionally. She grew to dress in a quiet, elegant style, and also learned that it was frequently better to listen than to talk. The high school preparation for the type of jobs that were available to women in 1949 was definitely on target for her.

On the other hand, during high school she had taken as many college preparatory classes as she could, and she followed up on that dream upon her high school graduation. She entered the University of Connecticut night school and took from two to four courses per semester every year until we were married and moved away. Her grades were exceptional: mostly "A"'s with just a couple of "B"'s. She took the advanced courses that were essential to the field in which she was interested, namely literature. She left the more general freshman and sophomore-required courses until later. She completed more than two year's worth of courses in college. In an English class, she was commended for her poetry writing. She always had the aspiration of writing poetry. Unfortunately, over the years, one particular notable poem that she wrote was lost, but as I remember, it was a good example of the use of the sounds of language to suggest and depict a point of view. It depicted the hissing sounds of the difficulties of life all around us, while we were safe in a glass jar looking out.

Her major field was English literature and she especially enjoyed Shakespeare and Old English works. I was surprised to learn that her long-term goals were to become a lawyer after college graduation. Unfortunately, due to illnesses later in life she never achieved that goal.

I would like to shift the story now and discuss my family and where I came from. My father, Herman W. Keeler, was born in Richmond and grew up on a small farm in Virginia. Through very hard work, he educated himself, obtained a bachelor's and a master's degree, did graduate studies in philosophical theology, and became an ordained minister with a thoughtful and philosophical view of the world and God. My own theological thinking and faith were

                                    Calvin Keeler, Sr.

strongly influenced by my father's deep faith and convictions. My mother, whose maiden name was Gladys A. Beers, was born into a minister's family in Canada, and became an accomplished pianist and organist. At the early age of about 20 she was asked to go on a piano recital tour, but declined, feeling that young women in those days did not do that sort of thing. She attended the Boston Conservatory School of Music. She always played the piano or organ at church for the rest of her life, and she played the piano at camp meetings each summer for forty years. My parents were married in Virginia in 1929. I truly have been and still am blessed by being born to my parents. I have been most fortunate in my life to learn from my parents to develop a faith in God, to develop discipline, to obtain an education, and to respect and take care of my body. Who I have become is in large part due to their efforts.

I have one sister, Ann, who became best friends (and maid of honor at our marriage) with Jane. Although Ann was about three years younger than Jane and five years younger than I, Jane and Ann talked on the telephone and at church frequently. If my memory is correct, I believe it was my sister who first suggested Jane's name to me in 1948. Sometimes Jane and I would double date with my sister and her date. Jane and Ann were close and remained close throughout the years. I am sure, to no surprise, that Jane and Ann worked together to arrange some of the dates from the first year of our courtship onward.

I believe that my life has been spared by

guardian angels for some reason. I remember, at the age of about five, being caught by a man just as I was racing my tricycle and could not stop, almost going right into Main Street traffic. I also remember losing control of a bicycle on an exceptionally steep hill and crashing at the bottom with my head landing just a few feet from a cement foundation for gasoline pumps. I remember another severe bicycle injury that caused a gash in my cheek that needed sutures at the hospital. I remember three very narrow escapes with takeoffs and landings on commercial flights over the years. At many other times, I have felt protected throughout my life when events occurred that could have caused me severe injury or death. I have also frequently felt strong guidance in many of my opportunities and decisions.

There was one major problem that Jane and I had to work through. Due to the desire of my parents to keep me single for several more years while I completed my graduate education, due to their desire to provide more direction to my future career, and due to the church issues previously noted between my parents and Jane's parents, my parents did not want Jane and I to marry. Right up until our marriage, they attempted to dissuade us (even on the day before), and Jane and I never felt the closeness with them that we desired after our marriage. At times it seemed like a problem, but the relationship that Jane and I had was too important to let anything come between us. However, family is family, and in spite of any disagreements with my parents, we shared with them in

                                   Calvin Keeler, Sr.

that love of a close family. I would propose that they just did not understand her yet.

Most fortunately, with my strong family life, I received a foundation in personal evangelical religion and an appreciation of music, history, and philosophy. I graduated from William Hall high school in West Hartford, Connecticut in 1948. I graduated close to the top of my class as I was in the top seven in my junior year. I received my bachelor's degree from Trinity College in 1951 at the age of twenty, when I completed four years of work in three including three summers, and graduated Phi Beta Kappa and with general honors and with honors in physics. I received my master's degree in mathematics from Harvard University in 1953, and then attended Harvard Divinity School from 1953 to 1955. I did not complete my divinity school degree due to Jane's developing illness, but have retained the dual interests of mathematics for my professional career and the study of systematic theology as a life-long avocation. My creator and my parents provided me with a strong body, which I have never abused and of which I take reasonably good care. I enjoy hard mental work and working with dedication and intensity. I have learned to discipline and apply myself, although I still have much more to learn.

I have very fond memories of my childhood and my teenage years. I remember all those services in church, singing good old gospel hymns, praying on my knees, and listening to my father preach and to my mother with her music. Moreover, Jane had those same wonderful memories of the importance of God in her life in church. We both learned to sit still in church worship services, more than once on every Sunday, from our first week of life as infants on. Fortunately, children's church or play time were not available in those years. It is also very beneficial that we learned to enjoy singing the grand old hymns about the revelation of God's love in Jesus.

Let me provide an example of how she applied her faith to others in her family. In 1951-1953, she brought her four to six year old niece to Sunday school and to church every Sunday. This action required that she leave her home by 6:30 AM to take several buses to a remote part of town to pick up her niece and to come back across town so as to get her to church on time. Then shortly after noon after services, she again spent over two hours taking her niece home again by bus. This niece became the flower girl at our wedding.

Jane's faith was so strong that whenever she went to one of her approximately fifty surgeries (twenty very major) and another forty serious tests and procedures, she never feared or worried. She knew that she was in God's hands, and that whatever happened, it would be His will.

Chapter 3

Just Married

1953 - 1954

After five years of courtship in 1953, Jane and I decided that we were mature enough to marry. I had received my bachelor's and master's degrees, and Jane had completed over half of the undergraduate work required for a bachelor's degree. We enjoyed each other's company so much that we did not want to be separated any more. We shared a mutual respect and total love for each other. When we were together, every problem seemed to be solvable. We did not reach our decision on marriage by blind infatuation. We were reasonably well educated, professional, disciplined, and mature in the world and religion, and wanted to live together while we finished our education. Jane wanted to complete her college degree and perhaps study law, and I wanted to do several years of theological study.

In the summer of 1953, I took Jane in a Model T Ford to get our marriage license at the city hall. The

Model T was borrowed from my sister's boyfriend. It was a typical Model T with spark advance on the steering wheel, manual choke, clutch, floor gearshift, and hand crank, which was sometimes used when the battery could not start the car. Later in life, Jane used to reminisce and laugh about how she went in her dress up work clothes to get our license in such an antiquated car. One usually dressed sportingly in such a car.

We set a date for a candlelight wedding at 7:30 PM on Friday September 11th, 1953. My father married us at the church in Hartford that we all attended. My sister, Ann, was Jane's maid of honor. My cousin, Reg, was my best man. Of course, Jane wore the traditional white wedding dress and was a beautiful bride with a beautiful smile. I think that we were each too scared by the importance and irrevocability of our decision to fully appreciate all of the wonder of the moment. We included an extra prayer in the service asking for God's blessing and protection of the family and home that we were starting. It was a beautiful ceremony.

The reception was held at the home of Jane's Sister, Eileen Bidwell, in Wethersfield Connecticut. We had some catered food and a wedding cake, but many desserts were homemade. We were fortunate to have many friends and guests attend to wish us well and on our way. It was good to know that we had so many friends.

Call it "destiny" or call it "coincidence," our marriage was truly an opportunity given to us and

Calvin Keeler, Sr.

provided to us by God. It was "meant to be" if only we would understand and accept it. I am so grateful that we responded and am amazed at how much our togetherness has changed and matured us over the years. We both felt truly blessed.

By the next day, Saturday, we were at our new apartment in Cambridge, Massachusetts. We were together for all time and nothing else mattered. Our honeymoon was to be spent setting up living in our new apartment, registering for school, eating two special meals out, and taking an overnight trip through the New Hampshire Mountains for the early fall foliage. It was perfect. Throughout our lives, we each felt that we were not just "soul mates," but that we shared a single consciousness.

Finding this place to live was another one of those things that "are supposed to be," or as some people call them, a "coincidence." It will shortly become clear why this was so important—this choice of a place to live later saved Jane's life. Sometimes, with our free will we appear to be led in one direction or another, if we will just remain open to guidance and intuition. We had spent one whole day in August before our marriage reading the newspapers and looking at the listings in the housing offices at both schools that we would be attending in the Boston area (Harvard University and Boston University) and could find nothing that was clean and not too expensive. I was ready to try another day. However, at the end of the day, Jane asked to go back to the housing office one last time, and she found one more listing.

We followed up and went to a large old house in Cambridge with a small cottage attached at the rear. An older lady, who was obviously well educated and cultured, and who had had a large and educated family, occupied the large house. She would not allow us to rent the small cottage until we had an interview with her son, who was a senior highly respected doctor at a large excellent local hospital. We returned to Cambridge a week later for the interview. We later found out that he approved of us because he especially liked Jane. The little cottage had two rooms each on two floors with a kerosene kitchen stove for heat. We furnished the house with a hand-me-down bed, kitchen set, couch, chairs, and cooking utensils. Jane had even distressed her very young niece when she had retrieved some discarded cooking utensils from an outdoors playtime sand box.

It is necessary at this point to recall some events previously mentioned. I have learned throughout my life that Jane had a profound effect on many educated and important people. There are three examples. In addition to the interview with the doctor just mentioned, let me remind the reader that the probate court judge took her particularly on his visits throughout the state to be his stenographer at probate hearings before we were married. As previously stated, he was very interested in her well-being and whom she intended to marry, and used his friends at my college to make sure that I would be acceptable. In another example previously mentioned, before we were married, her manger in the manufacturer's association took her to several meetings with railroad and trucking company presidents, where she made such an impression that one president tried to get her to date his son.

She was very serious, well spoken, educated, and gentle. She smiled easily, and was always properly and smartly dressed. Maybe it was something else, a look, the serenity of an angel, an aura, I just cannot say. I do know that she was the smartest person that I ever met, and that she had an instinctive clear vision of what needed to be done. Those such as Jane, who have a "presence," make a distinctive impression on those whom they meet.

She felt similarly about me. I was the smartest and nicest person that she had ever met. She adored me. Later, she told me that she was an "old-fashioned" girl, which meant that she wanted to take care of her husband, make him king, and to provide a good quiet home. Even later, when not feeling well, she got up every morning to fix breakfast and to send me out to work, when she could. And, when I came home, she always wanted me to relax and be free from stress. On the other hand, she was very modern, and it never occurred to her that she might have had challenges in becoming a lawyer in the mid-fifties. Had she reached her goal, I am certain that she would have had a remarkable career in her interests of children's and elderly law issues. Much of this came from her probate court work, but some of it came from early longings to help children who were disadvantaged.

My father loaned us his new car for our honeymoon while the car that we had purchased was having the engine rebuilt. After our honeymoon, we started our marriage with a 1937 Dodge. Today's drivers do not understand how cars of that vintage were usually in the shop for repairs more than once a month. There was always something: tires, brakes, brake cylinders, water pump, fuel pump, filters, alignment, points, battery (even had a battery fire once in this car), and the list was unending, especially for a couple on such a limited budget. As I remember, gasoline could be purchased for less than twenty-five cents per gallon. I even remember leaving a used tire as collateral once so that I could get gas to get us home. Later, I went back to make good.

On Saturday the next day after our wedding, I took Jane to the famous Boston landmark restaurant, Durgin Parks, where many world-famous people have eaten. In the afternoon after dinner, we drove north along the coast to Swampscott and Marblehead and bought some filet of fish for Jane to cook the next day for Sunday dinner. After attending church on Sunday morning, Jane attempted to pan fry the fish without a spatula. Even though all she had was a fork to turn it, I thought our first dinner at home was excellent and delicious. This was a testament to her culinary excellence that I was to enjoy throughout our married life. She was a really great cook, everything seemed so natural to her.

A couple of days later during our honeymoon, we took an early fall two-day car trip to the mountains of New Hampshire. The most memorable event, which Jane always remembered, was having a breakfast at a restaurant where we sat in front of a large picture window across the street from a beautiful tree, resplendent in the yellow and gold of fall, surrounded by the mountains in fall colors. The memory of the view remained with her always. She enjoyed her customary elegant breakfast of coffee, eggs, bacon, and toast. That breakfast menu was her favorite for all of her life.

The rest of that week was spent by each of us enrolling in classes for the upcoming semester. However, there is an amusing story concerning that. After four years part time at the University of Connecticut, Jane was transferring to Boston University. Since she had not received an answer of acceptance from BU, she made an appointment with the Dean of Admissions. When she asked him why she had not received an answer, he asked her to explain her poor grades. She then launched into a lengthy apology for the one "B-" that she had received. They soon realized that the University of Connecticut had provided the transcript of another person who had a similar name and who had received grades in the "C" and "D" range. Realizing the error, the Dean said that of course she was accepted and that she did not need to apologize for a "B-." They became friendly and talked whenever they met in the halls during the next semester.

On the next Friday, to celebrate the one-week anniversary of our wedding, we had dinner at the

Parker House in downtown Boston. She remarked later how pleased she was when I said to the waitress, "The pie is for my wife." She and I were very happy—we were together.

For the first time in her life, she was a full time college student, and she truly enjoyed the experience. We kept house together, but she was the cook. She carried her books on the subway to and from Boston University, where she made a close girl friend, and with whom we kept in contact for many years. She loved dressing like a college student and listening to college football games on the radio. For the first time, she had a college-level science laboratory class. On Saturday evenings, she often listened to Nashville country music on the radio.

We were together. We wanted to wake up together, to have breakfast and meals together, to share our daily lives, to study together, and to share our love with each other. This sharing of our lives sustained us through the many trials ahead in our journey. Fortunately for us, we had chosen the best way, for there was no other way that we could have survived and triumphed.

I have been very fortunate for all my years, except for my decision to marry, to have received total support from my family and had already accomplished a significant amount of formal education by the time we were married. Some thought that I was not marrying equal to my station in life. I believed then, and even more so now after a lifetime, that I married a better person, much more than equal. My

                                    Calvin Keeler, Sr.

very special married life of over forty-eight years is a testament to this. No one ever received so much love and true devotion from his spouse. She tried to make everything in my life easy and pleasant. She spoiled me.

For each of us, it was the best and the right decision, and we each knew it. We understood and fulfilled our destiny of supporting and respecting each other with love for our entire lives. In retrospect, I know that my life has been blessed by my wife and made much better, and I wonder why I deserved such a wonderful partner and where had she come from? Since I admire her decisions so much, I will have to accept the fact that she also found something special in me.

This issue of my parents' acceptance of our marriage became a problem between my wife and my family. I tried to reconcile the two sides for years with only partial success until much later in life. There were a couple of times when we did not visit, and there were times when I used all of my powers of influence and persuasion. However, I do believe that in the end my father in his final years finally understood her faith and strength. No matter how my family felt about my decision to marry Jane, we were still family and shared in the love of family. There is nothing more significant in this world than the love of family, and whenever we needed something, they were all there to help as much as humanly possible without limit. Without doubt, my mother and father each loved us.

As I am sure with most married couples, our first four months of living together were wonderful. Since we were both going to school, we had almost no money and thus lived very simply and cheaply. That was really OK. We enjoyed our studying together, eating together, going to school together, and learning to live together. To help with finances I took a part time job with an importing firm in Harvard Square, and Jane typed theses for graduate students. In our second year, I accepted a position as a teaching fellow in the Department of Natural Sciences at Harvard University. These activities kept us very busy.

From the moment of our marriage, our lives changed. Throughout our entire married life of over forty-eight years, we wanted to be together every minute of the day and night. Whenever possible, we always stayed in the same room. If something involved going to a different room to work, each of us just avoided that task at all costs. Except for cooking, Jane never went to another room. We studied together, I did my evening business work in the same room, I did my bills and taxes sitting near her, I prepared sermons in the same room, everything was done together. In later years, some thirty years later, when I had a computer at home, it too was in the same room, so that when I worked for hours on my computer, we were together. We just enjoyed being together. Evenings and nights were only tolerated when I was required to be at my place of employment, as were the business trips that I was required to take when I would be away. As long as we could be together and be holding hands, nothing else, even sickness, seemed to matter. Others have commented to me about how close and attentive we were to each other.

The major mistake of our first four months was mine. I continued to want to travel to both our families and to church each weekend from Cambridge, Massachusetts to Hartford, Connecticut. I guess I was trying to prove something to my parents. This became a cause for some disagreements between Jane and me, which we had to work through. Fortunately, later on this was resolved, as I became more mature. My wife began to be very tired with weekend travel along with all the study, and in retrospect, I suspect her body was already beginning to show some weaknesses from the diseases with which we would soon come face to face.

The first major signs of illness began to appear in January of 1954, just four months after our wedding. While Jane was studying for her semester final exams, she experienced bouts of severe stomach pain, nausea, and diarrhea, which lasted for several days. Obtaining a recommendation, we requested a visit by a local doctor who saw Jane in the home and pronounced it as "gastritis." He could not have known any better. My recollection is that the illness lasted about two weeks and prevented Jane from completing her examinations in two of the college courses. We had hoped that she would return to college for the spring semester, but as her weakness and illness continued, she just did not appear strong enough to register and start.

In February, she took a two-week temporary job in order to improve our financial situation. She agreed to clean out and organize an office of several rooms of scattered documentation so that a small group of scientists could begin a new company. It was very difficult and laborious work. She received congratulations on her efforts and results. Then by the first of March, she began a job as a secretary in the Department of Physics at Harvard University. She remembered one of the most senior faculty members testing her with almost meaningless technical and scientific jargon in a fake letter to see if she could transcribe it. She used dictionaries, catalogs, and whatever she could find to do the transcription. They were surprised and impressed at her effort and accuracy. It was only a test that she had passed. She was not happy. She made two close girl friends in just a couple of weeks in the department. However, within a month of starting this job, her life-long illness, which had been quiet for three months, began to reappear and overwhelm her.

Over the preceding couple of months, I had begun to understand how ridiculous it was for me to insist on travel to our parents' homes and to church each weekend, and we began to spend the weekends in our apartment in Cambridge. Fortunately, we began to separate ourselves from our families and to live our own lives.

For Jane, a home was a place of refuge and of

                    Calvin Keeler, Sr.

love. For our entire married life together, Jane always made our home comfortable and loving. It was a place where the family could meet together and find enjoyment and rest, separated from the storms of life outside. Her home was always beautiful and functional. It was a place where we all wanted to be and where we could all relax.

Vacations, special days, and holidays were always important to Jane. If we were home and by ourselves, she always planned and managed to do something, go somewhere, or cook something to make the day special. Many vacations and holidays were spent with our families, and we always tried to alternate the special days between our two families. Jane's family (parents, sisters, brother, and other spouses and children) was a fairly large group and always enjoyed gathering and having a good time, and Jane really enjoyed being a part of that. When Jane's family met on holidays, it usually meant a big feast with 20 to 25 members and required more than one table to be set up. There was always lots of special food, vegetables, and pies. They all enjoyed having a good time and being together.

Shortly after starting work in the physics department at Harvard and before any reappearance of her illness, Jane and I together decided to begin a family and to have a child as a specific conscious decision. This was about the middle of March. That was a wonderful choice for both of us and was easily accomplished. This decision occurred after she seemed to have recuperated from her January bout

with gastritis. We were totally unaware of the severe
illness that was about to develop.

Calvin Keeler, Sr.

Chapter 4

Illness Begins

1954 - 1955

For the first couple of weeks of pregnancy in March 1954, Jane seemed to be feeling well, and we happily told our parents our news. However, within a month Jane began to have severe stomach pain, nausea, and diarrhea. She began to become dehydrated and needed to use sick days at the physics department. We consulted with an excellent reputable Boston obstetrician, who was recommended by her affluent close friend in the department and who was also pregnant. Everyone was convinced for the next month or so that Jane's problems were simply "morning sickness." Due to dehydration, Jane required some short stays in the first few months in the hospital where the obstetrician was on the staff so that she could receive IV fluids and treatment. She also required one minor, but difficult, operation to remove an obstructing cyst.

By the early summer, Jane had had several

stays in the hospital and had become very thin, having lost a lot of weight, down to less than 100 lbs. On July 4th, Jane and I had a picnic lunch on a blanket near a lake a few miles from home. She was very weak, but was trying hard to be normal and not let anything get her down. They began to call her illness "hyperemesis gravidarum."

She was very ill and was vomiting several times daily. Her condition was serious, and no one in the medical arena had a clue as to the true cause. It was during this period that a family member complained in a disparaging voice that I "almost breathed for her." Although not intended as such, I did then and have always considered this a compliment! We just fought the illness together day by day, month by month, and year by year. While her sickness continued, I remained in my divinity school studies and in my teaching position. I spent the summer working at an importer for cooking ware in a nearby town.

It was decided by early August that Jane needed more prolonged specialized hospital care if she was to be able to keep her baby to the end of term. She was therefore admitted to a special maternity hospital, known then as the Boston Lying In Hospital. She spent about two months in the hospital (mid August to early October) because the staff was unable to find a cause or a cure for her condition of pain and nausea. Everything was tried, including extended psychiatric counseling, isolation from family and friends, and a variety of medical tests—all without result. She continued to receive pain medica-

Calvin Keeler, Sr.

tions, IV fluids, IV vitamins, and anti-nausea medicine. Nothing that happened to her in her illnesses at anytime in her life has ever caused me one moment's thought about reconsidering the rightness of our decision to marry.

The first anniversary of our wedding was on September 11, 1954. On that day, Jane had been in the hospital for about one month, and a severe hurricane was striking New England and Boston directly. Everyone was advised to stay off the roads, and most people did that. In spite of the warnings and the storm, I was one of a half-dozen visitors to drive, avoiding fallen trees, to the hospital to visit family and patients that day. I brought in pictures and other memorabilia from our wedding. We had become very close over the preceding year with all of her illness, and our day of memories brought us even closer. This was a very happy day.

It was during this time that she more fully developed her approach to sickness and hospitalizations that carried her through all of the difficult times throughout her life. In the hospital, Jane learned to relax and to let God touch her body and to let Him enable the body's natural healing functions, and to permit the medical staff to do their best to help her heal. In her hospital admissions, she was always patient and never anxious. She never worried about the outcome or whether she would survive. She endured every test and every needle puncture without complaint. In addition, in the mid-1950's needle technology was barbaric by today's standards: with rigid steel needles inserted into veins. Sometimes the attempts to access veins by this method could take several hours of trial because of traumatized veins and because that was the only technique available. Also, in this period medical staff usually tried until they succeeded, however long that might be.

Jane never complained. She always pictured herself as being released from the hospital and going home to get better. Truly being positive and happy, putting herself in the vision of being discharged better, and connecting with her eternal source and creator God appeared always to have beneficial results. These three factors in the previous sentence are three of the most important lessons that she taught me and are important for us to learn in this life. She just wanted to let her body heal so that she could get better and have the doctors send her home to her family. Interestingly, she made that exact literal statement to her doctors forty-eight years later in her final months on this earth while in the hospital. She told them she wanted them to "fix me up and send me home." That was always her only objective during every hospital stay throughout her life.

During the entire pregnancy, Jane and I were truly worried about the health and status of our unborn child. The gender was unknown, but Jane referred to him as "little Calvin." After the birth of her son, in order to differentiate between her two Calvins, senior and junior, she always called him "Calvin Lee." Up to the age of adulthood, he answered that his name was "Calvin Lee." We worried about birth defects and

      Calvin Keeler, Sr.

abnormalities that could have been caused by poor nutrition and/or the hospital medicines and drugs. With the current knowledge of this century, we now know that we had justification for worry. We were especially worried as Jane's weight continued to be seriously low. For most of her pregnancy, Jane was able to digest only minimal amounts of solid food. The only consolation that we got from the doctor was that a fetus is like a parasite and that it will always get whatever it needs from the mother.

I was very attentive to Jane. I tried, to the best that the doctors understood and explained to me, to provide the foods that she could eat when she was home. I tried to help her relax and rest. We know so much more about diet now, fifty years later. I rubbed her back or her forehead by the hour, which was about all there was that I could do to comfort her. One time I made a peanut butter sandwich in the shed so that she would not hear me scraping the jar. Most frequently, the nausea was severe, and every thought of food was disastrous.

In the last month or so of the pregnancy, Jane stabilized in her pain and nausea to a certain extent, and she was able to spend several weeks at home with short visits to the hospital for IV rehydration and nutrition and pain medicine. As her due date began to approach in mid-November, she again became dehydrated and had to reenter the hospital. During this hospital admission, our son, Calvin L. Keeler, Jr., was born at 11:08 P.M. on November 22, 1954 (almost full term). Her delivery process started about 8 P.M. and only took three hours. In 1954, fathers were forced to wait at home for news. Even though the obstetrician called me and said that both were doing well, I was very worried until the next afternoon, my first permissible visit.

For recovery, Jane was placed in a special room for mothers who had had birthing problems due to diabetes and other issues or when the babies had not survived. For several hours, Jane was not informed of the status of her newborn and was almost overcome with worry. By midmorning, she was told that the baby was normal, and then finally the pediatrician came by to reassure her. She was elated beyond words. When she first saw her new son, he was somewhat jaundiced and looked rather skinny. His birth weight was only 5 lbs. 9 oz., but that was a miracle considering what she had endured to this point. We gave thanks to God for his great gift and for his love to us.

Our struggle to overcome Jane's illness had become a strong collaborative effort. We tried to provide the kind of food that she could easily eat and that was nutritious. For all of the days and years of our living together, we always tried to get the right food and to provide adequate rest for Jane. Often, even with the best of intentions, she would get sick once more. I remember a few years later on one Thanksgiving Day when Jane was told that she could be discharged from the hospital, provided that she did not cook at home. We went to a very good, special suburban restaurant for a Thanksgiving meal. What

Calvin Keeler, Sr.

a mistake! It was too much, too rich, and too hard to digest, and she lost it before we left. A simple meal at home would have been much better for her.

Even now after she has died, I still wish I could have known then which diet restrictions might have helped her throughout her life as her illness progressed. The doctors were also struggling with the challenge to understand as medicine became more aware of the causes and effects. It is a question that we worked at with all of our efforts, and still only partially understood. Our failures were never for lack of trying. We were never too discouraged to try something new to make her eating and digestion better. The field of nutrition has had great advances in the first few years of the twenty-first century, which have not yet been taught to typical practicing medical doctors. I know that I now understand better how I might have fed and cared for her.

I became a student of practical medicine so that I could care for her. I watched her every breath and her every reaction to see how she was managing. I gave her intramuscular injections with narcotics for pain. I also gave her intramuscular injections of vitamin B12 and anti-nausea medicine. Of course, there were many pills to be taken at different times during the day. Fortunately, the pills in the 1950's do not seem to have had as many side effects as the pills of today. The doctors that treated Jane were very conservative, very attached to her, and provided a better treatment than a more aggressive path might have provided. We formed a partnership with all of her medical staff. I became Jane's advocate and voice, especially when she was too sick to communicate effectively or later when she was sedated in the ICU. Jane communicated very clearly to me what she wanted done. At times, I would do research in the Harvard Medical School Library and bring my results back to discuss with the doctors. Sometimes they would agree to try the suggestions from the research. In all cases, they fully disclosed to us the diagnoses, the possible implications, and the course of treatment.

In 1954, the customary hospitalization for childbirth was eight days, and upon coming home, Jane enjoyed taking care of her new baby although she was frail and tired. The doctors and the family were convinced that Jane's illness would disappear after the baby was born. When it did not, no one knew what to believe. Just before Christmas, my parents asked us to come and stay with them in Hartford, Connecticut for the holidays, as they tried to help. With any normal illness, such assistance would have had beneficial results. However, no one understood at that time what was wrong. We did stay with them over the Christmas holidays and, since Jane continued to have her problems with eating and pain, she was admitted to the Hartford Hospital for observation just before New Year's Day. After a week to ten days, the doctors admitted they could find nothing wrong and discharged her. So that I could complete my mid-year studies and exams, I returned to our home in Cambridge while Jane and our son remained behind.

Calvin Keeler, Sr.

Sometime later in January, I brought Jane and our son home.

Jane then spent two or three good weeks at home beginning to take care of her new baby and her husband. It was about this time that Jane and I were advised to have a night out. We left our baby with the wife of a student at the Harvard Medical School who lived on Beacon Hill in Boston. We needlessly worried so much that we were exceptionally glad to retrieve our baby after our evening out and to go home. He was very well cared for, but we vowed never to do that again. Therefore, ever after we never left our son with any one else except for close family members. The three of us went everywhere together or we did not go. At the age of two and three, it was customary to see our son dressed in a dress white shirt with a bow tie and a boy's suit, quietly sitting in the very best suburban Boston restaurants and eating properly. We ate out frequently, as often as weekly. We vacationed and played together, we went to church together, we shopped together, we were inseparable, and we all had a wonderful time. He felt very grown-up and special.

However, during the first week of February 1955 she visited with our landlady with whom she had become a very good friend, and had a chocolate. That chocolate precipitated a severe attack of pain and nausea that night. The landlady's son, Dr. Leland Littlefield, was the well-known doctor referred to earlier from whom we needed to obtain permission to rent the apartment. He came late at night and administered an injection for pain that he hoped would get Jane through the night. It did help some, and Jane rested for a little while. However, early the following morning the pains and nausea continued, and so we took her into the Mount Auburn Hospital in Cambridge by ambulance. That was the first of many ambulance trips that she would make to go to or from the hospital in her lifetime. There the doctor was an important member of the staff. Our next-door neighbor looked after our new son while my mother traveled from Hartford by bus to care for him.

At the hospital, Jane was placed on the danger list and received around-the-clock special nurses. Today this would have been called "critical care." Within 24 hours, Dr. Leland Littlefield, along with the chief of surgery Dr. Stanley J. G. Nowak, identified the cause of all of Jane's sickness. By external examination, confirmed with subsequent testing and surgery, they determined that the disease was pancreatitis. In the 1950's, pancreatitis killed its victims at least ninety percent of the time. The course of treatment was primarily blood transfusions, IV fluid infusions, pain medication, and anti-nausea medicine. Treatments that were more aggressive were usually counter productive and fatal in that era.

How fortunate we both were that these two doctors took her symptoms very seriously and did not ascribe them to a mental attitude, or to being depressed, or to being psychosomatic. It appears that Dr. Littlefield's previous relationship with Jane during the interview in 1953 helped them search for the truth rather than accept previous incorrect medical diagnoses.

Typically, gall bladder disease either accompanied or caused pancreatitis. About two weeks later, they operated to remove Jane's gallbladder and to remove as much infection and necrotic material from around the pancreas as they could. These conservative treatments were absolutely the correct response for that era of medicine. We would not discover the pathology and the cause for the pancreatitis until thirty-two year later, when it was proven that the pancreatitis disease was congenital. Fortunately, she did not become diabetic at this time. Enough of the pancreas was working to control her blood sugar properly. Later, beginning in the 1970's, she would become temporarily diabetic when her body was under stress as when she was receiving IV fluids with glucose in the hospital for rehydration and nutrition.

In 1955, hospitals usually only provided private rooms for patients with ample cash resources. Most patients were in wards. Jane's ward contained over twenty beds. The special nurse kept the curtain closed around Jane's bed, and the other nurses were also very attentive to her. I could visit her any time of day or night, and did just that. Jane's condition in the hospital was very grave, and she was asked, "What do you want to eat?" She replied, "A dill pickle," and the resident said, "Let her have it, since she is going to die anyway." When the chief surgeon learned of this event, he relieved that resident. Jane remained in the hospital for six weeks, proved the resident incorrect, and gradually got stronger, although the severity of the pain did not go away.

In an earlier chapter, I referred to some events, which are just "supposed to happen." Without any question, this combination of doctors in this hospital saved Jane's life, and we had been led there by the apartment listing that Jane had found late in the day when we were apartment hunting two summers previously, and which required an interview with the landlady's son, the doctor.

Further, during this time, we learned that we had earlier selected the right obstetrician because we were told that most other obstetricians and family doctors would not have permitted Jane to keep her unborn child to term with all of her medical problems, which did indeed threaten the lives of both Jane and the unborn child. We would thus have lost the joy and happiness of our son and his family. We were also informed that her poor health would prevent her from having any more children. Truly, we can say that God's hand was on us, and that He was working with us.

During this six-week hospitalization, Jane could not see her son. Thus at about five weeks, the private duty nurse walked Jane to a large window so that she could see me hold our son on my shoulder outside in the parking lot below. She always remembered our son on my shoulder and his little white peaked snowsuit cap. The doctors forecast that Jane would be an invalid for the rest of her life. In Jane's typical style and as became customary for her, she did not allow herself to become the expected invalid or victim, but used all of her energy to recover, to walk, and to become active again, so that she could go home after the six-week stay in the hospital to take care of her four-month old new son and her husband. She never let any illness get the better of her and always worked to live whatever life she could to the best of her ability. Her courage and strength in this regard has confounded parents, family, friends, and doctors over the years. The reserve upon which she called was truly not of this world. She firmly believed that not a moment of this precious gift of life is to be wasted.

During the month that she was home before her next hospital admission, Jane continued to have extraordinary pain along with nausea, which however was not quite as intense as before her operation. She was able to eat some. However, since she had such severe pain that did not respond to pills and treatment, it was decided that she would return to the hospital to have an operation to sever the nerves that carried the pain sensations from her pancreas. The operation was through her back and was called a left dorsal splanchtisectomy. One rib was permanently removed. The doctors freely admitted that this was a most dangerous operation for the 1950's and that the results were really in the hands of God. It was during this surgery that she awoke in the middle while being repositioned. This was the only instance of Jane awakening in all of her thirty or more surgeries with general anesthesia. She found it frightening, but fortunately she never let it bother her, and in all subsequent surgeries she just submitted to the anesthesia so that the doctors could do their job, help her get well, and send her home again.

She remained in the hospital for about a month after the operation, during which she gradually recovered as the pains and nausea both diminished. Her mother and I remembered one horrible time when the nurses and staff spent six or seven hours trying to find a vein for a needle, since the medicine of that era had no other alternatives. As she neared the end of the hospitalization, I brought our son into a satellite lobby for Jane to see and hold. Jane was disappointed because he was intrigued with the nurse's cap, and all he wanted to do was play with it. Then by May 1955, Jane returned home to care for her family and to resume as much of a normal life as she could. The pain and nausea did gradually improve over the months and years, although there were bouts when they returned. The doctors believed that she would never recover full mobility and would be a partial invalid. However, she just would not permit herself to do less than normal living.

At this point, I must comment on the rest of her extraordinary life. From these days forward, she never once had a day without pain, although for some days and periods they were less intense. Most fortunately for her, her body was able to use daily pain medications to permit her to live absolutely fully. Naturally, her tolerance for pain medication increased over the years, and many doctors and nurses were

	Calvin Keeler, Sr.

aghast at how much she could usefully use. Yet, I am able to say from hindsight that her pain medications never diminished her alertness or her quality of life. She tolerated her medications almost ideally. Of course, there were a few times over the years when she took too much medication, but never to the point of needing hospitalization for that. We never acquired or used any illegal medicines or prescriptions, but I worked the system to get what I believed that she needed. She also had a feeling of nausea and stomach discomfort most every day for the rest of her life, with frequent bouts of vomiting that might last for from two to ten days, with the most severe requiring hospitalization for IV rehydration and nutrition, and pain medicine.

As the months and years progressed, she continued to improve and brought up her son normally, doing all the things that a young mother would do. We took vacations, including swimming in the ocean day after day. She loved to clean her home, and it was immaculate, even though to her it meant dusting every room every day. She scrubbed her own floors until later in life. Nothing prevented her from living an absolutely full day every day, except for her sick days from time to time. She drove her car, went grocery shopping by her self, and shopped at the mall with friends. Later, when she worked, she held down her job and went lunching and shopping with her friends. We even used to love to walk about the smaller hills of New Hampshire every fall. In addition, church attendance was every single Sunday, except for vacation times. She was a fixture and a reliable standout in church, sometimes frail and pale and weak, but always there. Home movies show an active, happy, and smiling young woman, full of life and enjoying every minute of it.

There were days and even weeks over the coming years when her illness would confine her to bed, but she never let it get her down and out. She would stop the intake of food and liquids, then rally, get her strength back, and go back to taking care of her family and home, just as always. She just loved to cook, and she especially loved to cook for a couple of days before family company for holidays. She would cook several pies, breakfast rolls, cakes, appetizers, and all of the fixings. She just never ever quit, for life was just too valuable. In addition, she always made living enjoyable and fun. Life is to be enjoyed, since it is such a great gift. We had wonderful moments and days and years together. Whatever we did, we did together since we shared a single consciousness. Together we planned our vacations and trips, and we planned frequent outings to restaurants for the three of us from that first summer after the surgeries in 1955 onward. We both realized that life could be short and end at any time, and thus we decided to enjoy each day as it approached and not to wait to enjoy life in old age and retirement, or in future days and years.

Calvin Keeler, Sr.

Chapter 5

Living is Wonderful

1955–1960

In our first eighteen months of marriage, Jane had been hospitalized at least eight times. Right after her second major operation, Jane returned home in the late spring of 1955 and began to care for her family. Within a few weeks she was on her own while I finished another year of graduate level education. I remember that our mothers helped during the early part of this transition.

There had accumulated a significant number of medical bills, and we could see that Jane would need ongoing and extensive medical care for the rest of her life. Therefore as advised by our medical team, I left graduate school and accepted a position as a professional mathematician working on Air Force and NASA contracts in aerospace, cooperating with top scientists to discover the science of ICBM and space craft reentry. As a new family, we would need the monthly income and the employee medical insurance. This was a career that I would find to be satisfying and demanding, and that would also make a difference. Due to my new professional career in applied mathematics, my interest in theology then became my life-long avocation.

Jane's doctors told us that they expected her to have some significant incapacitation from the operations in 1955. At the very least, they expected her most recent operation, which involved surgery through the back along with the removal of a rib, might be expected to result in greatly diminished physical movement, including her ability for walking. She threw herself into normal living and caring for her family and totally avoided any and all incapacitation. She just willed herself to overcome all impediments.

She was told that her life expectancy was less than five years. That was unacceptable to her, and she informed me that she was going to live at least until her new baby was entered into first grade. She wanted to make sure that she cared for him during his early childhood and brought him up. She loved her son with the extreme love that every new mother has for her newborn, and she made sure that he was taught the best things in life very early.

Consequently, she immediately plunged into taking care of her family on all fronts in just a few short weeks. She enjoyed giving her newborn baby boy a daily bath, from which she had been prevented for five months. She enjoyed putting her baby son in a carriage under the trees and was ecstatic as her baby laughed aloud at the rustling leaves over his head when the wind blew. She believed that one should enjoy life to the best of one's abilities.

She forced herself to begin full participation in life. No matter how difficult, she accepted nothing less than full recovery. Sometimes it took a great deal of courage and fight on her part, but she was up to the challenge, and throughout her life, she always joined the struggle for full recovery. Until her final couple of years, she was always able to return to the full care of her family, for that was what life was all about.

In the summer of 1955, she began again to cook meals, to clean the house, and to do some of the washing. We started taking a few small rides, the three of us, around the neighborhood. In the middle of the summer, we took our baby to a large beach in the hot sun just north of Boston. Our baby was well covered and with a sun umbrella to protect him. She truly enjoyed all the little things that one does just to live. At this point, she was still very skinny, and so she purchased a small number of clothes in the smaller sizes. Throughout her life as her sickness came and went, she would lose weight and then regain weight. Thus, she always needed clothing in multiple sizes available in the closet for all contingencies.

By the end of the summer, she was able to walk by herself to the nearby grocery store and to other shops in a nearby city center. She even took our son in a stroller shopping with her on several occasions.

The doctors informed us that Jane's eating and diet would need to be carefully controlled. She was told to eat nourishing lean foods, such as homemade beef stew. Over the years with the assistance of the doctors, we learned more about the dietary restrictions that her type of pancreatitis would impose. At the time, all that we knew was that she should eat lean, low fat, and non-spicy foods. We got better as time went on at knowing just what Jane could tolerate as we learned from daily experience. The downside of learning and not really knowing up-front was that from time to time she would experience severe attacks of pain and nausea from her pancreas due to her food choices. We never fully understood the reasons for these onsets, but we got accustomed to having attacks. Often, even while following a very strict diet, and sometimes while on just liquids, the nausea attacks occurred without any knowable cause.

As the fall drew nearer, we became concerned about our one-year-old baby crawling on the floors of an attached cottage during the winter heated only by a kerosene stove in the kitchen. Therefore, we moved to a five-room apartment on the second floor in a town nearby. Jane took the move very well and quickly adapted to our new home. She continued to do all the work of caring for her family, such as meals, washing, cleaning, and taking care of her son. She read a great deal and loved to read the classics and Shakespeare. Our son would sometimes sit

                                    Calvin Keeler, Sr.

in her lap and ask her to read from her books rather than from his books. They would sometimes walk together to a nearby library and charge-out books, where he would say, "shhh." These were precious days and full of life.

We had stopped our weekly trips to Hartford in the winter of 1954 due to Jane's oncoming severe illness. After the operations in 1955, we resumed occasional trips to both of our families in the Hartford area from time to time. She enjoyed the driving and stood the traveling fairly well, as long as we did not stress her body too much, and we allowed her time to recover from all the other events of life. When we drove, she was always relaxed and confident of my driving. During these younger years and especially at night, she would lie on the front seat and nap on my right leg. In later years after many illnesses, she could no longer lie on the seat, curl up, and have a nap. Then, she sat next to me, watching the road and my driving, enjoying every minute, and talking with me without any complaint. Even when almost an invalid in later years, and during very stressful trips of four hundred miles from Delaware to the hospital in Boston, she enjoyed sitting next to me and calmly watching. It just felt right.

During this year in the apartment, she did not let any of the constraints from the sickness of the prior two years be an issue or a factor. She cooked a hot breakfast of bacon and eggs frequently, and enjoyed cooking hot dinners with meat and vegetables. Our very young son loved to call out, "More bacon" at breakfast. Then, she would laugh. I remember New Year's Day 1956, when she invited her school girl friend and her husband from Boston University days over to a large New Year's Day dinner of roast turkey. Nothing was going to keep her from living a full and complete life. I remember that once we drove through a blizzard of eight to ten inches of snow to a grocery store, almost just for the thrill of doing it in a storm. There were no issues that would stop her from being young and happy.

She routinely took the washing out to the back porch and put it on a reel clothesline. Unfortunately, once while doing this, she fainted and almost fell over the railing. It frightened her, and she tried to be more careful. This was just one more reminder of a general weakness that she was constantly fighting to overcome. She let our son help her load the washing machine and made it play time. We began to buy furniture and the other necessities for keeping house. She enjoyed a pantry full of dishes and utensils, and she and her son would cook and bake together with flour and other ingredients in the kitchen. One time when she could not find her son at first glance, she found him in the cleaned and unused fireplace, sitting by himself and acting as though he were reading a book.

After about a year in this apartment we moved to Ithaca, New York while I took special courses in numerical analysis and aeronautics, which were related to my profession. This lasted for three months as we lived near Cornell University. Jane, her

                                    Calvin Keeler, Sr.

mother, and our son flew to Ithaca and stood the trip well. It was Jane's second air trip and her mother's first. Jane enjoyed the time in Ithaca, but as the weeks passed, physical problems began to accumulate, and so we realized that she was not ready to be separated from the extensive care network of the doctors who knew her so well back in Cambridge, Massachusetts. We were pleased to remember for years that we had eaten at a very fine restaurant at Cornell University in Ithaca.

We returned to the Boston area by car. Upon return, Jane continued to see the doctors who had cared for her in the hospital in 1955. She required monthly visits with frequent adjustments of medicines. Naturally, the medicines in the 1950's were much less potent than the medicines of today. During this period from 1955 until 1959, she saw her doctors frequently and, by my recollection, required a couple of hospitalizations in the 1957 - 1959 period for IV rehydration, nutrition, and pain medicine. She continued to try to live a full life and just would not accept any physical restrictions from her disease.

We, of course, always tried to maintain close control of her diet, since it was quite obvious that when we did not, she did get very sick. Even though we lived within the rules the doctors gave us for Jane about eating, I recognize from the perspective of today just how important diet was and what additional controls would have been better, had we but known them. Being Jane, she loved to cook and bake, and loved to eat good food, such as roast beef, turkey, ham, fish, vegetables, pies, cakes, breads, etc. Adjusting to her diet was not a problem for her since it was good wholesome food and fit well with her lifestyle. Other than her diet, she just never wanted to accept any other limitations, but to live her life in a grand and enjoyable style.

From the time that our son was born in 1954 until the early 1970's, Jane and I were blessed by having two families that would help us whenever she was sick. Whenever she would start vomiting and be required to remain in bed or whenever we moved, one of our mothers would come and spend several days with us to help take care of Jane and our son. I do not know how we could have made it without them. Sometimes they were there with us for weeks at a time with only a few days off on weekends. Thus, I could continue with my job. Occasionally Jane's sickness would persist a day or two, but typically the illnesses lasted a week or much longer. Whenever we called for help, one came. Furthermore, one was always there to take care of our son whenever Jane was in the hospital. Once, Calvin Lee brought Jane's mother her suitcase and asked her to go home, saying that whenever she came, mom seemed to be sick. He did not understand that causality.

Upon our return to the Boston area from Cornell University in late 1956, we spent about half a year in a first-floor apartment. Being near her doctors, she did improve and enjoyed a fairly good time. In early 1957 with the help of Jane's sister, Eileen, we purchased our first new home, a six-room cape, in

Calvin Keeler, Sr.

Wakefield, Massachusetts. Jane was overjoyed. We lived in this house for two years until early 1959. In spite of several major sicknesses, these were wonderful years for her. She really enjoyed taking care of her son who was three to five years old while we lived there. This house was a dream to her, and she enjoyed furnishing it.

Two things that she did were to obtain her drivers license to go grocery shopping by herself, and to join the choir at the Wakefield Congregational Church. She used to drive herself to choir practice on Thursday evenings even during winter storms, and she sang in the choir every Sunday morning. She had an alto voice. She found a good girl friend in the choir, and they had good times together. As the income from my profession improved, we began to eat out more regularly at restaurants.

Having moved back from Ithaca to be closer to her doctors who had recently treated her, she received regular medical care to keep her health as strong as possible. Our home was a two-story cape, and on those days when she was sick and vomiting, she would stay on the first floor in the den near a bathroom. Occasionally she would faint. One time when fainted, Calvin Lee placed a wet facecloth on her forehead until she revived. That was a fond memory for her. These events never appeared to adversely affect him because they were just a normal part of life, and he was always very close to his mother. She did not complain or make an issue of these problems for him. Further, Jane always encouraged him to watch for me to come home from work and constantly praised me to him. Thus, he was able to combine his love for his mother and me. I remember that each of our mothers again visited us several times to care for her. I do not recall any significant operations during this period, but I am certain that she was in the hospital once or twice for IV rehydration, nutrition, and pain medicine.

We bought rugs, dining room furniture, and kitchen furniture, and fixed the house quite nicely. The house was on a tree-shaded lot with green grass, and she planted flowers and bushes around the house. The house was on a dead-end street so that there was no traffic. We sent our son to a day care school at the age of four so he could play with other children. After a couple weeks he came home and told his mother, "Tell Daddy to save his money because I am not getting an education. All we do is play." We let him stay home with his mother.

We bought a freezer and filled it full of good food from a freezer plan. She enjoyed months of good steaks and roasts. For the most part she was stronger, and her life was much more enjoyable. When I received a good job offer from an aerospace company in San Diego, California, with substantially greater pay, we decided that she was strong enough to move and explore some new experiences. We, therefore, packed our furniture, sold the house, and moved to California, where we settled in a rented five-room ranch house in San Diego. I drove by myself to California, while she flew on one of the first transcontinental jet flights from New York to Los Angeles with our son. She did remarkably well for this three leg trip from Hartford to New York to San Diego. Our families despaired to see us go, thinking that they might not see us for some time.

Due to the fact that Jane's disease was very infrequently identified in that era, we were unable to find the right kind of medical help in San Diego, and it became obvious in a little less than a year that we would need to move back to the Boston area. She also had some minor health issues due to climate change and vegetation allergies. They were difficult, but she worked through them. We were not able to find a physician whom we trusted, and those whom we contacted made wild suggestions. She also said that the direct sunlight on her head felt much hotter than she liked. We enjoyed swimming at the beaches, we enjoyed going to church every Sunday morning, and we enjoyed eating at two very fine restaurants regularly. Our son went to kindergarten and was the standout since he was the only one paying attention and not just playing during the Christmas pageant. I took a few flying lessons. We became close friends with one of our neighbors, and they took my son and I grunion fishing at the ocean beach once.

My work required that I take several trips to the Boston area during the year to work with a subcontractor regarding missile systems. Jane and our son flew back with me once and once by them-selves. During one such visit back to New England, she spent several weeks with her mother during her father's hospitalization from a heart attack. Except for the ongoing medical problems in San Diego, this was a good year for Jane, and we were glad that we had made the change, but only for a year. Due to her long-standing medical condition, we just could not remain there for an extended period of time. We drove back to Boston by car, taking about eight to ten days. On the way we stayed overnight in Las Vegas and took in a show. When a little more than half way back, Jane got very tired, and we needed to hurry our trip along.

Calvin Keeler, Sr.

Chapter 6

Making the Most of It

1960 - 1970

After a year in San Diego, I received a good job offer from a small company back in the Boston area. We had a short stay in a furnished apartment suite in Cambridge, and then moved in 1960 into a rented split-level house in Winchester. We stayed there for a little more than two years. We both became very active in the Winchester United Methodist Church and sang in the church choir. Later, after our son grew to the age of fourteen, he also joined us in the adult church choir as a tenor. Because of my theological study, I taught Sunday school and became a local licensed preacher in the United Methodist Church for the Boston Conference. I remained in ministerial support activities in the New England area for almost thirty-five years.

In 1960, our son entered first grade in a very unusual private school, called the Bartlett School, which proudly used teaching methods from the early twentieth century and before the more modern changes in school curriculums. He spent five of the six years of elementary schooling at this institution, and received an outstanding primary education, which allowed him to enter one of the finest prep schools in the Boston area upon graduation from the sixth grade.

We bought rugs and drapes, and furnished our home. Jane drove herself for shopping and to church. The only major car accident of our life occurred here while I was driving. We were broad sided at an intersection with all three of us in the car. The driver of the other car told the police officer that he had not seen any light, let alone the red light. We were shaken up and were checked out at the local hospital with no injuries other than bumps. The car had a lot of damage.

Sometimes Jane would shovel during the winter snows, and even tried to break ice from the street drains to relieve the small floods that occurred at the dip in the road in front of the house. During one such winter flooding from the snows, the garage was flooded and we lost many boxes of memorabilia and pictures.

Upon our return to the Boston area from California in 1960 and throughout the decade of the sixties, Jane willed and forced herself to live just as normal a life as possible. She truly enjoyed taking care of her family and cooking, she enjoyed her housework, she enjoyed our trips, she enjoyed going shopping; and she enjoyed her church work. She enjoyed the beaches at Cape Cod in the summer and the fall foliage trips in New Hampshire, Vermont, and Western Massachusetts as well. We visited both of our parents and our sisters from both families in the different states of New England. Anyone who saw her in any of these activities would believe that she was a happy young girl, and full of life. Yes, she was truly happy and full of smiles, as we can view on our old home movies.

From about 1961 until 1969, we traveled to Cape Cod, Massachusetts, for summer weekends and vacations. Jane's sister and her husband, Eileen and Dan, built a summer home on Cape Cod. During the construction, which took over a year, Jane and our son, Calvin Lee, spent many summer weeks and weekends with them on the Cape in the partially constructed house. They had a wonderful time together—roughing it, going to the beach, eating, and just plain laughing. If Eileen and Dan were busy, then Jane and I would rent a motel room on the Cape for the weekend or the vacation days. Even when it rained and stormed, I could not keep Jane and our son out of the water. They just loved it. I do not believe that we missed many vacations or summer weekends from these recreational activities during this period.

During the period 1961–1963, while we were

living in Winchester, she had several attacks of pancreatic pain and nausea, expressed as continuing severe abdominal pain and gastric problems with dehydration. Because of the periods of sickness, she would lose weight and become thin. Upon regaining health, Jane always enjoyed eating good food and would regain the weight that she had lost. I believe that Jane had one or maybe two major abdominal surgeries during this period at the Mount Auburn Hospital in Cambridge. Her pancreatitis was atypical and confusing, but some hospital medical tests and her symptoms continually reaffirmed the diagnosis, which had previously been verified by surgery. In each case, she endured a three-hour surgery where the surgeon would examine the pancreas and try to remove any necrotic material and inflammation. The surgeons also explored the duodenum and the ampulla of Vater (and sphincter of Odi). Since the pancreatitis was not typical and since they could not find a more permanent cure, the doctors became a little discouraged in their diagnosis and treatments. Some less accomplished doctors even doubted the diagnosis. However, the doctors continued to treat her diligently to enable as full a life as possible. And, Jane did not disappoint them.

On many Sundays for over a year, we invited the student assistant minister to Sunday dinners, and Jane enjoyed putting on full meals of roast beef, vegetables, salad, rolls, and pie for dessert. We always ate well and enjoyed good nutritious food. We did not eat junk food, and we were careful to avoid spices

     Calvin Keeler, Sr.

and greasy food. The assistant minister enjoyed playing tidily winks with Calvin Lee on the living room floor during meal preparation.

Although we lived in a split-level house, Jane was able to negotiate the stairs fairly well and was very careful about her footing. She enjoyed going grocery and clothes shopping, enjoyed going to choir practice and church, and enjoyed vacation trips. During this period, our son was in the first and second grade. She immensely enjoyed playing with him, watching TV with him, playing outside with him, sliding in the snow, and shoveling snow with him. She always knew that he was "special," which is what he really turned out to be.

During this decade, our financial situation became more typical. I held a job that involved mathematical and computerized modeling, consulted in project planning and review techniques, and was assigned for several months as the manager of a large data center dedicated to astrophysical research and associated with Harvard University. In the evenings, I consulted in advanced programming techniques for aerospace industries, solving mathematical problems.

Due to the state of the economy and the company with which I was employed in 1962, I became aware that my career opportunities were becoming limited. Therefore, I found a new position as the manager of data processing with the aerospace company that I had previously worked for from 1955 to 1959. I stayed with this company at several different management positions until 1972, when a combination of an economic slowdown and a reduction of the aerospace/defense industries caused me to again look elsewhere. The major problem with accepting this new position in 1962 was that it required a family move to a new facility in Tulsa, Oklahoma. This new facility was situated fairly close to NASA in Houston, Texas, and we expected to do significant business with NASA. After a lengthy discussion, Jane and I agreed that she was strong enough to make the move, having been told that there were excellent medical facilities in Tulsa, and she looked forward to the change.

Jane and Calvin flew to Tulsa, while I drove the car. We did find a good medical internist doctor in Tulsa, but Jane's problems continued and became more difficult for us to handle. She was admitted to a very good hospital once during our year in Tulsa for about 10 days due to pain and the necessity for IV rehydration, nutrition, and pain medicine. During our year in Tulsa, we purchased a very comfortable air-conditioned seven-room ranch home with two bathrooms. The extreme heat of the summer bothered Jane, since our car was not air-conditioned. Air conditioning in autos was still relatively rare in 1962.

Jane and I joined a large United Methodist Church in downtown Tulsa and became choir members. We attended church regularly. In Tulsa, the whole family enjoyed eating extraordinarily good quality beef, which is typical of the area. We took a few trips into the countryside to visit gift shops on reservations. During the year, our son enjoyed another very excellent private school, Holland Hall, for the third grade, and he began to learn to play the violin.

For the first time in our lives, we were able to afford domestic help to assist Jane with ironing and keeping the house clean. We developed a very fond relationship with this person and were able to share some noontime meals together. Our helper was surprised to be included to the point of being invited to offer grace when we had lunch together.

As during our other previous move away from New England, we made several short trips back to visit our relatives, sometimes coordinated with my visits to the Boston area offices of my firm. In 1963, I became aware that Jane's condition was again worsening and requested relocation back to the New England offices of this aerospace company where we would be closer to her doctors. The company graciously accommodated this request.

After the move, we lived in Cambridge in a rented furnished efficiency apartment for about five months until we were able to move into our new home. During this short time, Jane was again in the Mount Auburn Hospital, where she had already spent so much time, at least twice for IV rehydration, nutrition, and recovery. During her visit to the hospital in October 1963, the builder came to the hospital so that Jane could pick out wallpaper coverings and fixtures. To prevent another admission, we had even tried subcutaneous intravenous fluids at home under a doctor's supervision, but without much success. Jane's next visit to the hospital was in early December, just before we moved into our new home. In December 1963, we moved into the home that would become our residence until August 1999, over thirty-six years. Jane really felt that she had good roots for this whole time.

Our new home was a split-entry ranch in Lexington, Massachusetts, and was a very large house in one of the nicer, executive-level suburbs of Boston. This home was much more than adequate to support my later executive management positions. On the main floor, there were six rooms, and on the lower floor, there were three more rooms. There were two fireplaces and three bathrooms, a much larger house that we needed, but it was in a very nice area with many trees and was on a very quiet residential street. My mother was with us on the day that we moved into this home, and she knew that Jane had just been discharged from the hospital the day before. It was a little overwhelming, for Jane just wandered around the boxes. The next morning Jane was fine, and we settled very quickly, as she adjusted and really "dug in," as was her custom.

Jane charged into being a homemaker with great enthusiasm. She immediately began a pattern, which would last for decades. She dry mopped the hardwood floors daily until we purchased wall-to-wall rugs a few years later. After the rugs were installed, she used her vacuum cleaner at least once per week. Until she became too ill, she also dusted her tables,

   Calvin Keeler, Sr.

knick-knacks, and other surfaces each and every day. Of course, she kept immaculate bathrooms.

We had a hi-fidelity system (a very old fashioned phonograph by today's standards), and she would always put on some classical opera, symphony music, or gospel music at top volume, filling the house with music, and just work harder than any one I know at cleaning her whole house. She knew how to get the dusting and cleaning completed happily, quickly, and without complaint. She enjoyed these times.

With a large, well-appointed kitchen, she enjoyed cooking for several hours at a time more than once a week. This lasted during our entire residence in Lexington. She could cook anything and tried and modified recipes as she went along. When making pies, she would make at least two different kinds at a time. In addition, for many years she baked her own bread. Her cookbooks were well worn, as she prepared meal after meal for us. Each and every supper (even for the two of us after Calvin left) was always a full meal with meat or fish, potatoes, vegetables, and desserts.

We returned to the United Methodist Church in Winchester as active members, and rejoined the choir. With my interest in theology and church work, I renewed my activities in the ministries of the church.

In the late 1960's, she held a choir party with all kinds of goodies. Sometime during this same period, she threw a Thanksgiving party for thirty-five of her relatives that included appetizers of chips, dips, sliced cheese, fruit cup, fruit punch, shrimp, grapes, and other fruits. Her dinner was two turkeys with five or six vegetables and hot rolls. Moreover, the desserts included at least three pies, a coffeecake, and a regular cake. She was an absolutely perfect cook, and would try anything. She loved to eat and enjoyed all of her own meals, as well as eating out at restaurants. Fish or shore-side restaurants were especially desired. If it was not fish, then she wanted the best steak or roast beef. It is ironic how much she enjoyed eating, while having to be so cautious of what she ate, and of the dire implications if she did not follow her diet. Almost all of the time, she found the correct compromise, so that eating was always pleasant and a fun thing. Meals, at home or out, were always happy times.

Our yard, which was a normal suburban-sized lot of about 12,000 sq. ft., had thirty or forty trees, including several large oak trees. Raking leaves in the fall was always a big project. We planted shrubbery around the house. Jane and our son planted several flowerbeds at obvious points. She enjoyed working around outside. One spring, I dug up, and she and our son planted a large new flower garden out back. We went away for the weekend to Cape Cod, and when we returned, we discovered that the rabbits had eaten everything, except for a few coarse stalks.

During the decade of the sixties, our summer vacations were usually at the beach, where we all enjoyed swimming and beaching. Towards the

                                    Calvin Keeler, Sr.

end of the decade, I began to notice that long periods of time on the beach were becoming more difficult and tiring for Jane, so I started to look for other recreational alternatives. I decided to purchase a small sailboat and learn how to sail. The first year was a learning experience and so was not very comfortable for her, but she enjoyed every minute with smiles. We progressed in 1970 to a 20' larger cruising type sailboat, which had cushions, a head, and a stove so Jane could nap and be more comfortable.

Every fall the family always took trips to the mountains of New Hampshire and western Massachusetts to view the fall foliage. This was always a highlight of our fall season and was sometimes overnight. We used to enjoy walking in the leaves in the big forests.

In the mid-1960's, Jane developed a bleeding duct in her left breast. The surgeon at Mount Auburn Hospital who did the original diagnosis of pancreatitis removed the duct. There was no disfiguration and no further repercussions of any type.

In approximately 1966, Jane had another abdominal surgery on her pancreas, which slightly improved her condition, but which the doctors felt was unproductive. The skilled doctors who had saved her life in 1955 were now less involved in advanced surgery and were retiring. Consequently, the doctors at the Mount Auburn Hospital recommended that we seek medical help from a larger hospital where the doctors had national reputations and were involved in more research. Thus, at about this time, we transferred care for Jane's pancreatitis disease to the Massachusetts General Hospital (MGH) in Boston Massachusetts. Shortly thereafter, she spent approximately forty-five days under observation at the MGH so that the doctors could get a better understanding of her general condition and how her illness affected her living. We were most fortunate to have the chief surgeon of the hospital, Dr. George Nardi, take care of her until his death in 1988. Because of his unusual expertise, which included specializing in pancreatitis, and his extraordinary gentle and kind manner, he even willingly took care of Jane medically during times when we did not have a primary internist on the case. We were fortunate that no doctor ever removed her pancreas or took overly aggressive research steps that would have shortened her life until medical science could do so safely.

In March of 1968, we decided to take a quick vacation to Florida, our only vacation trip to that state. I had been under great stress, and we thought that this would be good for us all. We drove to Vero Beach by the end of the third day and stayed there for three more days. Jane and Calvin had a really great time, swimming and eating in fancy restaurants. It was very restful for all of us, and we enjoyed it immensely. The drive home did tire Jane out considerably, and it was difficult for her, especially since I did not stop one last time for the night when we were about six hours from home, but pressed on. If I had kept each day's drive to a reasonable maximum, it would have been better for her.

In the late fall of 1968, Jane had a subtotal hysterectomy to solve some other problems. This operation was very successful, and there were no further problems there either. Because her veins had been used so extensively over the years, an experimental procedure was used to provide IV fluids. A stainless steel "T" was sewn into her left jugular vein. There were no problems with this procedure but it certainly foreshadowed the dozens and dozens of central line insertions that she would have in later years, and due to scarring, precluded the use of that site later for a Hickman central line insertion.

Jane and the entire family were surprised and saddened by the sudden death of the oldest sister, Lois, on December 21, 1968, in the hospital from a severe case of the flu. She was buried on the day before Christmas. Just a few months later, the third oldest sister, Winifred, died in the hospital on March 1, 1969, after open heart surgery for the replacement of a heart valve. This type of surgery was quite innovative at that time. The family told me that they would not have been surprised had Jane been the one to die, but everyone was shocked by the other two deaths so close together.

Chapter 7

The Good Years

1971 - 1986

The period of sixteen years, from 1971 to 1986, provided Jane with many very happy memories. Even though she was in the hospital more than twenty times during these years and even though she had several major surgeries, some of which were life threatening, Jane believed that she should daily live her life to the fullest. She was grateful for each day and understood that whenever she saw the doctors or was admitted to a hospital that she would get better and return home to her family. She accepted every procedure without complaint, just knowing deep inside that God was with her and that her body would heal. Without exception she always expected to spend a few days, endure procedures, and return home much better.

For approximately two years, 1969 - 1971, she held a job as a computer programmer in the local aerospace company where I was employed. She drove her own car, went for lunches with the girls, played cards at noontime with us guys, and went shopping by herself. Towards the final few months of her work experience, she began to get weaker, to struggle, and to get sick again, and it became clear to me that she would need to stay at home to conserve her energy and to enjoy her life. She was never well enough to work again.

Our son graduated from the Belmont Hill prep school in 1972, and she was happy and proud to be there for the ceremony. He was a member of the school glee club, and she enjoyed attending the recitals at Christmas time during his six years there. He next entered Tufts University in 1972 and graduated with honors in 1976. The happiness of his graduation was sobered for her when he left home permanently soon thereafter in order to attend graduate school. The day after he left, she sat in his room and cried for most of the day. Some years later in 1986, he again made her very proud when she traveled to Maryland to be there for the awarding of his Ph.D. in microbiology. However, as the years had progressed, she had become weaker, and the travel to see him receive his doctoral degree was difficult for her. Since his graduation and post-doc experience, he has become a respected full professor in microbiology at the university.

Calvin was a perfect son, and the respect by each of the three of us for each other was mutual. The three of us had been inseparable, and our relationship was the envy of those who knew us in church,

Calvin Keeler, Sr.

in sailing, and in the family. Since each of us was always respectful of the others, each of us enjoyed our time together. We enjoyed and laughed at every meal together, whether at home or out in restaurants. He studied hard and received excellent grades. He never got into any trouble of any kind or had any major arguments with either of his parents.

He took his faith very seriously and attended church and choir at all times joyfully without any complaint. He became an outstanding driver. When away at graduate school, our phone conversations were frequent and caring. No one could ever have wished for a better son. One family member stated that she did not want to be around if something happened to any one of us. With his travel away to graduate school in 1976, the breakup of our daily close contact began, although gradually at first. Even when separated by distance, we have remained very close. We have continued to remain close and caring for each other, and with our strong support, Calvin began to add other priorities as he started his own family and established his own lifestyle.

Not only were Jane and I protected by guardian angels as has been already reported, but I can also recall at least three or four occasions when our son was protected by God from certain injury or death, just as we had been. In all these cases, I am sure that our lives were spared because there was something else that God has wanted us to do, and He has given us that opportunity.

I took Calvin to several major league sporting

events (baseball, basketball, football, and hockey) over the years in the Boston area. The three of us vacationed together, went to the best restaurants together, and went to church together. Yet, Calvin was his own person and became a very strong individual in control of his own life. For him also, the first day when he was fully separated at graduate school was difficult, and he remembers it, but it was a very necessary and growing experience. We have both always been immensely proud of him and his accomplishments.

When we were first married, Jane wanted to have six sons. However, she was able to have only one child. She told me that the goodness of all six was wrapped up in the one son, Calvin. He, therefore, was the recipient of all of her love and efforts. All of her dreams were thus bound in the life of Calvin, and he never ever disappointed her. As she said, using an old expression, we "put all the eggs in one basket."

She fed her family elegantly and shopped at special butcher shops and vegetable stands so as to provide the freshest quality food. Her recipe repertoire was extensive, and some recipes were her own modifications and creations. Our family always had a hot meal at suppertime, except for fancy dinner salad meals in the hot summer. Often in New England in the wintertime, we would get major snowstorms of ten to fifteen inches of snow. On those afternoons, she would cook supper, keep it warm, and then stand in the window to watch for her family to come home and lovingly welcome them. Even more, she loved heavy

Calvin Keeler, Sr.

snow days, when work and school were cancelled, and the whole family would be home together.

She created new recipes and just naturally created new dishes. The meals were very nutritious, using fresh vegetables, fresh fish, and excellent cuts of meat. All three of us had better health because of her cooking skills. She had a real gift and aptitude for cooking. After dinner, she always tried to get me to leave the kitchen and to relax after a hard day at work while she did the dishes. She was very efficient and quick in the kitchen and in her housework. There was never a crisis at mealtime, as all her tasks were well planned and executed. I cannot remember any problematic or poorly cooked meals.

We loved to go to the best restaurants in the Boston area, from downtown to the suburbs, for the best and freshest dinners of fish, including lobster, roasts, and steaks. During the summer, we were accustomed to eating at restaurants several times per week, and in the winter at least once per week. We always went first class.

In 1972, we transferred our church membership from the United Methodist Church in Wakefield to the one in Lexington, our new hometown. We became active members in the Lexington church and remained active until our move to Delaware in 1999. Throughout the years, we formed very close relationships with each of the ministers appointed to the church, and each of them visited Jane regularly whenever she was in the hospital. Over the years, in addition to my local licensed preacher activities, which included preaching several Sundays during the year at our church and at others, I was also involved in many administrative functions at the church. We formed lasting friendships with the members of this church. Whenever Jane was not in the hospital or on vacations in the summer, she never missed a Sunday at church.

We were known for walking down the aisle to our seat hand in hand and for usually holding hands while we sat. We did not attend church dinners, since she had such eating issues. In church, she sat tall and straight and always exquisitely dressed in an elegant and cultured, yet quiet style. She loved the music.

Wherever we went, we always went hand in hand. We held hands at the mall, when grocery shopping, when entering and leaving restaurants, at church, at the yacht club, and whenever we went anyplace together. One student minister with whom she became friendly gave her a book with the title "Hugs."

She knew how to dress. She just knew which colors went with which. She preferred simple styles with colorful accessories. Some friends remarked that they just wanted to get into her closet for five minutes. Much of her shopping was done by catalog. She had the ability to visualize how a dress would look on her, and she was usually right, both as regards size and color. There were very few returns. She loved to shop by catalog, and this was one of her pleasures that I encouraged. She really enjoyed shopping at the mall, when she was able. When it came time to

                                   Calvin Keeler, Sr.

buy party dresses for the executive office Christmas party, she knew exactly what to buy. She would be gorgeous and in excellent taste.

In the 60's, she had begun to go to a hairdresser salon occasionally. By the 70's up until almost the end, she would go weekly. She liked a faint reddish tint to highlight her natural color, and wore her hair very sedately and stylishly, loosely curled close about her head.

She purchased all of my ties, and every morning except on Saturday, she selected the summer or winter suits and ties that I would wear. I have never known anyone who could purchase and match ties so well. When we were in the men's stores, I needed her assistance in selecting my suits, pants, and other clothing. She was much better at it than I. She wanted her family dressed properly, just as she did. Without her skills present in my life today, I have difficulty in making the proper selections. However, she did leave me a great assortment of ties from which to choose.

She furnished our homes in the same elegant and quiet style. Her curtains and drapes were absolutely perfect in style and color. She liked them plain and without wild flowers. They had embroidered designs, however. She preferred light rugs (close to champagne color). She liked a bright and cheery house with lots of sunshine. She picked out very durable, yet functional and sturdy furniture, which would last in an executive-style home for years to come. She liked large sofas and several large comfortable chairs in the living room. In the bedroom, we had a king-sized bed and large and heavy dressers and tables, with a lounge chair. I purchased her a large grandfather's clock for her birthday in 1975, which she just loved. She had curio cabinets and knick-knacks discretely placed, including memorabilia. The entire home was extremely well appointed. Jane made our home a refuge from the struggle in the world and business, and a haven to provide healing from illnesses.

One of Jane's highest pleasures and goals was to take care of her family at home and then send them out to shine and to be successful.

I have never known any one with such an eye for propriety, color, and elegance. Whether it was clothes or furnishings, she had an instinctive feel as to what would be elegant, quiet, and properly color coordinated. She never selected wild colors or big floral patterns. Her friends would tell me that when they went shopping, Jane could just enter the store, stand back, look at several racks of clothes, and pick out from a distance the one or two items that would be good candidates for purchase. When it came time for the final selection, my friends said that she just knew which one would be the best. They liked to go shopping with her and envied her skills and judgment in this area.

As mentioned earlier, in 1970 I upgraded our first training sailboat to a larger 20' cruising boat, and in 1972 began mooring it during the summers in Marblehead Harbor, Massachusetts. In 1973,

I upgraded to a sturdier 26' sailboat with larger bunks and head. From 1970 until 1996, when we sold our cruising sailboat, we spent the majority of our summer vacations on the boat in the harbor at Marblehead. Most of the time, we took small day sails around the area, rarely venturing very far away. Frequently Jane would lie down and rest while listening to the swoosh of the water past the boat in the gentle breezes. She found the boat very restful and recuperative. Often we just stayed in the harbor at the mooring and talked and watched the birds, and the waves, and the other boats as they came and went in and out of the harbor. In retrospect, this was an ideal way for Jane to get away from home, to get some fresh salt breezes, and to relax. I have never regretted the time we spent together in Marblehead Harbor. Often we would eat a good fish dinner ashore at a local restaurant in the evening. This lifestyle was very recuperative for her.

We bought a multi-colored kite in the form of a windsock that we flew from the stay wire at the stern whenever we were on the boat. The many colors swirling over our heads in the breezes and wind were reminders of the good times that we had whenever we were on the boat, whether we were sailing or just resting in the harbor. I still have and cherish that kite.

Jane's job on the sailboat, which she loved, was to go forward, past the shrouds to the bow of the boat, and then to pick up the mooring and attach it to the mooring cleat as we entered the harbor and reached our spot. I usually furled the sails and started a small gasoline engine outside the harbor to improve my maneuverability in the harbor. In spite of her physical limitations, she clambered forward and did this clear up until our final year of sailing in 1995.

In 1972, I bought a racing sailboat, called a "Daysailor," for our son. He was on the sailboat racing team at college. It was a little less than 17' long and was equipped with a lot of racing gear. He and I raced together more than once a week every summer thereafter, in addition to racing in competition both in Marblehead and in other locations at regattas. We raced in several national events and in Marblehead's summer race week series every year. We were competitive and while spending our summers racing together, became the envy of the other members of the fleet for our relationship. Calvin was the skipper and helmsman, and I was the crew.

When we would return to the harbor, Jane would be on the larger cruising boat watching for us and waving to us, hoping that we would reenter the harbor first, which often meant that we had won. Calvin and I always sailed up to the boat that she was on and around it, before mooring our racing sailboat. In the evening on race days, the three of usually had a fish dinner at a seaside restaurant and, of course, talked sailing. Sailing with our son Calvin, Jr. lasted until 1977, when he became too busy with graduate work in a different state. Upon a few occasions before he left, he would take his mother sailing when the winds were very gentle, and they had wonder-

                                                        Calvin Keeler, Sr.

ful times together. The memories are precious. She happily told me about how he pointed out to her the cats paws of the wind on the calm ocean surface and how thrilled she was when they passed other racing sailboats.

In 1984 an unusual event occurred. I had traveled by air to Omaha, Nebraska for three days on business. So that Jane would not be alone, I had taken her to visit her sister Eileen in Connecticut. One night at 1:30 A.M., I woke up and sat up with fright and an overwhelming sense of fear. It seemed to me the Jane was calling to me that she was afraid. Without using a telephone, I spoke to her and said that everything was OK, and that she could settle back to sleep. When we talked on the telephone the next day, she confirmed that she had awakened with a terrible nightmare at 1:30 A.M. She also confirmed that she knew that I had said it was OK, and then she settled back down to sleep.

During her adult life, there were many days when Jane did not have nausea, and more days without vomiting, but there were almost never any days in which she did not have pain. One of the reasons for being admitted to a hospital usually included the necessity for injections of medicine for pain. Sometimes the doctors permitted me to give her injections for pain at home. On other days, she used pills to alleviate her pain. Many residents and unseasoned doctors were shocked about how much pain medication Jane could tolerate, but the occasions when she had too much medicine for pain were infrequent and far between. She was always cogent, alert, and able to carry on intelligent conversations. It is said that if one has a lot of pain, then the medicine given for pain alleviates the pain and does not affect one's abilities and alertness. Such was the case with Jane.

Every couple of years during this period there were occasions when her pain and nausea became so severe that Jane required hospitalization at the Massachusetts General Hospital. The attacks continued to increase in severity with increasing pain and dehydration, which resulted from her deteriorating pancreas. Several major abdominal surgeries were attempted to relieve these symptoms. However, these attempts were met with only temporary and partial success. The technical aspects of the operations were also becoming more difficult, since by this time both her gallbladder and spleen had been removed, alternate connections to the duodenum and small bowel had been attempted, and there was scar tissue everywhere. The total number of major operations had by this time reached at least twenty since the diagnosis of her pancreatitis in 1955.

By early 1985, Jane's overall medical condition was becoming grave again. She was almost continuously ill and weak, and getting weaker. The ongoing complications of illness were taking a severe toll. She was becoming debilitated and the strength to continue life was diminishing. Our summer vacations had ceased. On December 24th, the day before Christmas, in 1985 Dr. Nardi decided that medical care for diabetic patients had advanced to the point where she could survive following the removal of her pancreas. In the year 1985, December 24th was on a Monday and was treated as a semi-holiday at the hospital. Therefore, Dr. Nardi had no operating room scheduling pressure in taking as long as he needed to perform the surgery. Jane spent a full eight hours on the operating table.

When the operation was completed, the doctor came to me and told me he was uncertain as to the effectiveness of the surgery since there had been so much scar tissue that at times he was unable to determine exactly what he was cutting. Part of the risk of the operation was the fact that, even with his world-class skills, when some of the scar tissue was cut, the procedures had caused interruptions in some blood supply to the intestines, which then required further resections of the small and large bowel. Later colonoscopies determined that the small bowel had been modified to attach to the large bowel just before the descending colon with a side-by-side attachment. X-rays later also confirmed that sections of the small and large bowels had been bypassed and were not passing and absorbing food.

Jane spent three days in intensive care, and it was difficult for me to see her so sick. She fought the intubation and the ventilation on the respirator, and did not easily adjust to the breathing rhythm. Calvin traveled from Delaware to be with his mother and me for support, which was appreciated. His words to his mother helped her to adjust to the breathing rhythm. Even though I had watched her illness up close for thirty years, I was unprepared for the struggle and difficulty she faced. Eight hours of surgery is a major insult to the body. I was able to observe it very closely.

Within a few days it was determined that glucose levels were close to normal and that she would not require routine insulin injections. She did not become a diabetic and require insulin until 1994, except for times of stress due to rehydration with glucose and fluids in the hospital. We therefore determined, as was later proven by further scans, that the islets of Langerhans, which secreted insulin and controlled the levels of glucose in the blood, had not been removed since the surgeon had been unable to separate the tail along with the body of the pancreas. This part of the pancreas remained functional. It was also later determined by further GI studies that a portion of the head of the pancreas was still attached to the duodenum and had not been removed. This surgery was an amazing technical feat and is a testament to the skill, courage, and determination of an outstanding surgeon, Dr. Nardi, and also to the facilities at the MGH. Without the skill and determination of the surgeon and without the best-of-class facilities, Jane would not have survived. And survive and get better she did. It was almost beyond my comprehension.

The dissected pancreas was submitted to pathology for study, and the results were informative. Examination showed that the major duct, the duct of Wirsung, was not obstructed, as is customary for pancreatitis. The problem was that there were obstructions in the capillaries and small ducts leading into the major duct. This explains why the standard tests for pancreatitis, including the ERCP, were not always effective in diagnosing the problem, even though the symptoms of pancreatitis had been present from the beginning. The conclusion from this pathology study was that her pancreatic illness had been a congenital condition, and which had become life threatening in 1955.

During the following year, the surgery healed, and Jane progressed and continued to get stronger. I believe that she required the assistance of IV nutrition in the hospital once during the year. However, the severity of the pain and the severity of the nausea were sharply diminished. The operation was a total success. In 1986, she needed surgery to remove some cysts and a fistula from the area of the surgery. Following this latest surgery she continued her improvement.

Jane faced her illnesses with a strong faith. She was never aggressively outspoken to her medical and support teams about her faith and beliefs in God, but she had said enough that they knew from where her support came. I know that her faith carried her through all of her troubles. Of course, she confirmed her faith with our ministers when they visited, and she appreciated their prayers for her. If anyone else asked her if she believed, she would respond positively, but she never challenged anyone else, since they had a right to their own beliefs in peace. Once, a hospital aide, who was working in her room and who had come to know her, gave her a lapel pin of an angel, and told her that the angels were watching over her. Jane said that she knew that, and proudly wore that lapel pin on her coats for the rest of her life. She was blessed in her faith and believed that God's angels did watch over her. Many ministers said that she gave back to them more than they gave to her. Some would visit her several times per week while she was in the hospital.

Jane was a favorite patient for the chiefs of surgery at both the Massachusetts General Hospital and earlier at the Mount Auburn Hospital. She was fortunate to have the best of doctors take a special interest in her, and in her faith and desire to live a normal life.

At my office parties, she also attracted the interest of some presidents of the companies where I worked, and sometimes they would request that we eat at their table, while she and they continued to chat. Even during her short stint at the Physics Department of Harvard University, she made an impact. She always made an impact. Moreover, of course, she made good friends with her co-workers, several of whom mentioned how much they admired her. One male friend wished that I were not around. She made several good and close friends over the years. One special friend, Jean Santelmann, in Lexington in the 1980's and 1990's, as will be shown later, gave her an outstanding compliment and honor. She was always a great asset to everything I did.

Since I did so much to care for Jane, and since

I had become Jane's spokesperson and advocate, my understanding of medical science and care was, of necessity, growing. I studied all that I could find on the medical issues that concerned Jane. I spent time in the medical school library, and taught myself to be reasonably conversant, so that I could more fully understand the conversations, diagnoses, and proposed course of treatments with the doctors. Over the last eight years of her life, I needed to learn many additional nursing skills so that I could perform them at home.

In 1988, Dr. George Nardi, the surgeon and doctor who had cared for her since the mid 60's, died from cancer. Just before, Dr. Nardi asked an outstanding internist and endocrinologist at the MGH, Dr. John Godine, to take over and to continue the care for Jane. Dr. Godine was tireless and skilled in his efforts to solve Jane's medical problems for the rest of her life. Jane and I formed very close bonds with both Dr. Nardi and Dr. Godine.

In 1983, Jane's father died after a long illness. Many years earlier, he had had a heart attack. However in 1983, after a long siege with Alzheimer's disease, he had another heart attack and died in the hospital after general organ failure. Jane's sister Eileen had cared for him at her home for many years. Jane was strong enough to travel from Massachusetts to Connecticut for the funeral.

In 1986, my mother died in the hospital from a heart attack several months after a severe stroke. Previously, my sister Ann and my father had cared for her for several months at home. Jane was not well then, but, in order to attend the funeral, did travel to Connecticut and stayed with Eileen. She made a great effort and was able to attend the funeral. I officiated at the funeral, and was supported by my wife and our son, who traveled to the funeral from Delaware. My father, my sister, and I planned and coordinated the services and meal.

Chapter 8

Succeeding in the Struggle with Illness

1987 - 1998

The proof of the success of the surgery to remove the pancreas is evidenced by the fact that Jane exceeded forecast expectations and lived for almost seventeen years after the surgery, but with ever increasing effort. They had hoped that she might have at least five years. For many years, she was able to live nobly and with great dignity. There were, however, several admissions to the Massachusetts General Hospital from 1986 until 1994 for malnutrition where they prescribed TPN (total parenteral nutrition), given by IV for rehydration and nutrition. The severity of the pain was under control, and normally eating good food resulted in fairly good nutrition in spite of poor food absorption. In between the hospitalizations, she was able to enjoy life and live well. However, too often out of the blue, eating and nausea were still problems, which were what necessitated the hospitalizations and the TPN. Overall, these were very good years, but with declining general health, and greater and greater effort on her part.

In October 1988, Calvin married Sharon Brown in Wilmington, Delaware. Jane and I traveled to Delaware for the ceremony and the celebrations. In the photographs, Jane looked very pale and weak, since she was still recovering from recent surgeries and ordeals. Nevertheless, this was a happy day for us, and we were pleased to have Sharon become a part of our family.

From 1987 through 1995, Jane had a good life and enjoyed doing many things. At least once or twice a year, we traveled to Delaware to visit Calvin and Sharon, and similarly they traveled to Massachusetts to visit us. During these years, except for the visits to the hospital, Jane's life appeared normal. Every Saturday she had her hair done, and every Sunday she went to church. During the summers, we spent weekends and vacation weeks on the boat, sailing near Marblehead. In the fall, we always took our annual trip to New Hampshire and Vermont for fall foliage, and at Christmas time she was a knockout at the executive Christmas parties. She was also able to participate in many family holiday festivities.

In the late 1980's, she developed cataracts in each eye. In the course of a little more than a year, she had surgery to each eye to remove the cataracts and insert implants. She recovered spectacularly from

  Calvin Keeler, Sr.

these surgeries. Within a couple of years however, the ophthalmologist noticed deterioration in Jane's retinas and transferred her care to a retina specialist. She was diagnosed with the beginnings of macular degeneration. Probably because of poor absorption, treatments with vitamins did not work for her and did not appear to have any beneficial effect on the retinas. For the rest of her life, that is, the last dozen years or so, the macular degeneration continued to worsen every year, until by the year 2002, she only saw in the most peripheral edges of her retina. Yet, she never complained, never commented that she could not see, enjoyed every fall foliage season, and just adjusted to her eyesight so as to enjoy living normally, savoring whatever vision she had left. The ophthalmologists had expected the deterioration to stop at several different plateaus of vision along the way, which did not happen.

So that she could enjoy her cooking in the kitchen, I entered several of her favorite recipes into the computer and printed them in very large type. Thus, she could read and follow them by herself. She always enjoyed cooking. She just never quit in any part of life.

She was declared legally blind. Yet, she hid her condition so well that unless tested, the medical care team and others could not tell that she could not see well. She made do with her peripheral level of vision, even as it was diminishing. She never made her eyesight a problem and refused to do less than enjoy all of life.

In 1989, we traveled to Delaware to celebrate the birth of our first grandson, Timothy. This was a short visit for Jane, and Jane always enjoyed traveling by car. She looked forward to each trip up through 1995. In 1988, we had bought a new Mercury car that had a cassette tape player. She acquired several cassette tapes, many given to her by Sharon, with pipe organ, classical and religious music, and we enjoyed playing them in the car tape system for each of our trips. From then on for the rest of our trips by car, we always listened to music as we drove. Sometimes we would start back late and not arrive home until the wee hours of the morning. Although tired, she always looked forward to these trips to be with our family.

In 1994, Sharon and Calvin presented us with a second grandson, Jeremy. We were able to fly to Delaware for that joyous occasion. We have been very happy with our two grandsons.

For someone who did not like baseball at the age of sixteen on our first date, she always urged me to watch sports on TV and to attend sporting events around Boston. She said that it helped me to relax, and she always thought about what was good for me. I was able to take her once to a Red Sox baseball game at Fenway Park in Boston. We sat in the 600 Club, which is an up-scale enclosed area behind home plate where we could eat a meal at a table and watch the game.

In 1996, as her eyesight was deteriorating, I bought a larger 30 inch color TV set so that she could watch it better. The large screen allowed her peripheral vision to see more, and satisfied her right up until the end. She enjoyed having the TV set turned on.

During this period, my income had increased rather significantly, and thus I was able to indulge Jane in one of her favorite activities. Since breakfast out at a restaurant had always been a real treat for her and as it was her favorite meal out, we visited a different restaurant all over the greater Boston area every Saturday morning for breakfast for several years. Of course, we did develop some favorites. We tried the very elegant, the good, and the average restaurants and hotels, both in the downtown financial district and all the way out to the suburbs. She enjoyed each one, and she looked forward to getting dressed each Saturday morning as a special event for the two of us, just talking gently together and looking very much in love. She was always just full of smiles.

Sometime either just before or in 1995, I took her to our favorite well-known suburban Boston fish restaurant for an anniversary dinner. I ordered her a cup of clam chowder and a 2 ½ pound boiled lobster for her dinner. I cracked and fed her the lobster. She had the best time, just full of smiles and laughter, as she enjoyed eating every bite. Her happiness is a wonderful memory that I will always cherish. We shared many smiles and happy days almost back to back. Even in the hospital, she constantly smiled at every member of her care team and at the medical staff that visited her. She was known to be never grouchy or hard to be with, even at her sickest.

In spite of the rather frequent admissions to the hospital during the years 1987 to 1994 for TPN, we enjoyed wonderful years. She always ate good nourishing food, but too often, there occurred a bout of nausea, with resulting loss of weight and the beginnings of malnutrition. Jane had exceeded the life expectancy forecast of five years following her pancreatectomy in 1985, but her digestive system had sustained just too much damage. Her future was beginning to turn bleak with more frequent hospitalizations and ever increasing weakness. A major milestone was reached in 1994 when the medical support team at the MGH, during another admission for dehydration, proposed placing Jane on home-administered TPN. TPN is a liquid solution containing vitamins and the elements of nutrition necessary for life. Many patients with severe digestive problems live on this for years, and even travel (as did Jane) taking the TPN, supplies, pumps, and equipment with them.

There were several results and/or consequences from the implementation of this suggestion. First, Jane's quality of life was much improved. She no longer had severe cases of nausea—which resulted in malnutrition and required hospitalization—as her nutritional needs were fully met by the TPN at home. Eating became a pleasant, although unnecessary act. She ate for pleasure and to satisfy natural hunger feelings. During the better times, she received the TPN four nights per week and during the sicker times seven nights per week. Ordinarily the TPN ran eight to twelve hours per night beginning in the evening and ending each morning. If she felt an attack coming, she just stopped eating and relied on the TPN.

Secondly, I needed to learn a great many nursing protocols, since I had to complete the final preparation of the TPN solution and also care for the Hickman central line, which was implanted into her clavicle veins. The major components of TPN were mixed in a sterile lab and then sent to the home in plastic containers. Later, when the central line became infected and the clavicle vein became occluded in the hospital, the Hickman central line was placed in her right jugular vein. I learned how to keep the site sterile and how to change the dressings every couple of days. It was necessary to keep the Hickman central line itself sterile. I learned how to administer the TPN with a pump at a prescribed rate and how to modify it as the prescription changed. When she had major infections, I was directed to give her IV antibiotics through her Hickman port, which I did many times, including before dental work. Finally, I learned how to draw weekly blood samples and deliver them to a blood lab, so that the nutrition and other important metabolic levels in her body could be properly monitored.

Thirdly, in spite of the insulin which I added daily to the TPN bag because it contained glucose-rich TPN fluids, Jane became a full diabetic, and we needed to routinely monitor her blood glucose levels and to inject insulin from two to four times per day. She rarely complained about the pain of testing her blood sugar, which was done by pricking with a sterile lancet to get a drop of blood, even after extensive testing over the years had caused her skin to become tough and necessitate multiple attempts to get the drop of blood.

Fourthly, in 1995 we saw the beginnings of the deterioration of Jane's immune system. No matter how careful and sterile one might be, the lab preparation and the subsequent administration of fluids intravenously on a daily basis, month after month and year after year, subjected the body to infections. This is true even in the best sterile hospital environments.

Fifthly, recent research into nutritional science has shown that natural whole foods contain the best sources for vitamins and minerals to support the immune system. Continual usage of glucose fluids and synthetic vitamins has also been reportedly shown to frequently cause a weakening of the immune system. It appears that one should not totally replace foods with TPN, unless there is no other recourse, and then only if one recognizes and accepts the long-term implications. It was the infections and illnesses from the breakdown of her immune system over the next eight years that finally ended her courageous struggle. It is amazing that she had the strength, the courage, and the will power to endure that long.

In mid-1995, Jane had a staph aureus infection that required hospitalization with the surgical cleaning of her right wrist. This was the first of many examples of a weakening immune system. Her right

                                    Calvin Keeler, Sr.

wrist had been very swollen and painful. She survived these treatments well and recovered the full use of her right hand. Some years earlier, she had had a broken left wrist from a fall at a conference in a poorly lit building, and then as at this time she continued to use her fingers in peeling potatoes, cooking, and doing all the tasks around the house while in a cast. Thus in both cases when the casts were removed, there was no need for therapy, since she had already recovered the full use of her hand. She never let herself stop working to be and keep well.

For Thanksgiving Day in 1995, Jane invited her sister and husband, and our son and family to our home for Thanksgiving dinner. She was getting very sick, and I was concerned that we should not continue with the holiday preparations. She insisted that the holiday celebration proceed and cooked the usual turkey with dressing, vegetables, and pies. After the visitors left, it was obvious in the next few days that she was seriously ill and struggling to even move and to be functional.

On December 1, 1995, I finally convinced her and took her to the emergency room at the Massachusetts General Hospital. She was gravely sick and was immediately admitted. It was quickly discovered that her body was being overwhelmed with the fungus candida. Her illness was so severe that in the nine and one-half month period from December 1, 1995 through September 15, 1996, she was home only three times with an approximate duration of one month each. In early December, she was treated with amphotericin and fluconazole for the fungus and infections. Within a few days and due to the infections, she needed the Hickman central line changed. During the procedure, she contracted a VRE infection (Vancomycin resistant enterococous). The VRE infection stayed with her for the rest of her life and required private room isolation for every hospital admission thereafter. Nurses at home and in the hospital were required to follow isolation non-contact procedures, since VRE is one of the new super bugs for which some of the weaker and sicker patients in a hospital setting have no defense and no cure. Jane was able to tolerate the medicines required to keep it in check, but she was never able to completely eliminate it, even though tested routinely.

Within a few days, Jane developed a very severe pain in her neck and spine. X-rays and CT scans were taken which showed that the candida had crossed the barrier and entered into her spinal column and had caused at least one abscess. This was called fungal osteomyelitis, and it is extremely rare for candida to progress from the body to within this protected area. The pain and discomfort from CT scans and other treatments was excruciating. On December 7, 1995, her neurosurgeon was examining her in the evening as she was beginning to lose feeling in her feet and hands. He immediately recognized that the blood supply was being cut off in her spinal column by an expanding abscess. Since the transport personnel were taking too long to come, the doctor and I then pushed her bed to the operating suite. He imme-

                    Calvin Keeler, Sr.

diately started surgery and performed a laminectomy, removing the posterior of C3 through C6 cervical neck bones to reduce the pressure of the abscess. Since the surgery was going to take four hours, he advised me to go home, as Jane would be going from surgery directly into the neurosurgical ICU.

I went home, and later the neurosurgeon called to report that the operation was a success. I am sure that the stress contributed to make me feel very tired. Therefore, I went to bed and went sound asleep. At 12:30 A.M., I sat up with a feeling of sheer fright and felt that Jane was calling to me in a panic. I reached for the telephone and called the nurse's station at the neurosurgical ICU. I asked them if Jane had just entered there from surgery. They said, "Yes," and wondered how I knew. I told them to tell her that I would be there in half an hour, and so I quickly dressed and drove to the hospital. They were still working on her when I arrived, and I was unable to see her, but she knew that I was there and she tried to relax in spite of the respirator breathing machine and all of the other equipment that was attached to her. I saw her in an hour or so. This is another example of how even distance did not separate us. We could hear each other when in trouble across the miles.

The stay at the neurosurgical ICU was very difficult for Jane because she experienced an extraordinary amount of pain. After a few days, she returned to her hospital room, where she stabilized. For the remainder of the month of December, she remained in the hospital with a great deal of pain up and down on her spine. Clearly, the candida had been eliminated from the majority of her body but not from the spinal column, where they discovered more spots of inflammation and small abscesses.

Just before Christmas, we began to be optimistic as it appeared as though she were beginning to get stronger and improve. However, between Christmas and New Year's it became clear to all that her condition was again deteriorating, and the doctors requested CT scans and an MRI. On December 31st, the neurosurgeon announced that her cervical spine was deteriorating further, and he was concerned that the bones in the neck were greatly weakened and might crumble, and that her head might fall off to one side.

On the next day, New Year's Day, January 1, 1996, the neurosurgeon performed a cervical fusion, totally removing C5 and C6, and replacing them with bone fragments from her hip. The cervical bones that were removed were infected, soft, and collapsing. With this type of operation in 1996, a fixed halo was attached to her skull with four pins into the skull bones and an upper body brace to keep her neck absolutely immobile for 90 days. Medical science has currently developed new techniques and procedures that are less invasive than the ones used in 1996. Again, she was sent to the neurosurgical ICU with a breathing ventilator for a few days.

After this operation, I made a decision, which affected both of our lives for as long as she lived. I decided that I would spend each night with her when

   Calvin Keeler, Sr.

she was in the hospital and not leave her alone. That way, I would be there to take care of her when she needed help, needed to be comforted, and was unable to call for the nurses. She really did need extra help, since she was unable to care for herself. The nurses took note of my decision and admired our devotion to each other. The nurses still smile about it when I see them. Until I retired, I would spend every weekday night and the entire weekends with Jane, leaving early in the morning on workdays to go home to dress for work, and returning to the hospital in the afternoon after work. After I retired, I always spent the entire day and night with Jane, leaving only for meals, usually in the hospital cafeteria, and to go home, or to a local laundromat for clothes washing every week or two. As long as we were together, nothing else ever mattered. We both believed that we could endure anything, as long as we were together.

We talked a lot and smiled, just being in each other's company. I held her hand and comforted her. I held her in my arms a lot, and kissed her gently. When her IVs stopped or when she needed help, I would call the nurses. When the doctors arrived for rounds at 6 AM, I needed to be awake to discuss her condition and course of treatment. When she was getting MRI tests, I sat in the procedure room with her with the MRI machine to help her through the long tests, since she found it very difficult to hold still for so long. She was never alone, except for my quick meals. For many of her ambulance rides to and from the hospital after that, I was with her. When being admitted through the emergency room, I was always there with her. When in intensive care units, I stayed with her from early or mid-morning (as permitted) until late evening, holding her hand gently, even while she was sedated, to let her know that she was not alone. The nurses permitted it, understanding how much it helped and that we truly were inseparable.

As previously noted, due to the fact that Jane had a VRE infection, she required a private room so as not to infect other patients from this time forward. In one hospital, I was able to use a small pullout couch in the private room for my nighttime rest, and in the other hospital, I used a sleeping bag on the floor. Whenever she called, I answered. In 1996, she spent six of nine months in the hospital, and I was there every night. In 2000 through 2002, she spent fourteen of her last twenty-two months in the hospital, and except for when she was in intensive care, I spent my entire days and nights with her.

The three months in 1996 with a halo and neck brace, and even the following six months, were very painful for Jane. Rev. Susan Morrison, who was the minister at our Lexington United Methodist Church, visited Jane extensively during this period in the hospital. On some days, Rev. Morrison visited with her for several hours, and for some weeks, she spent several days with Jane. Rev. Susan, as she was called, attempted to help Jane to cope with the pain by prayer, by meditation, and by relaxation procedures. Her help was invaluable in those difficult days.

Calvin Keeler, Sr.

Two months following the cervical fusion and one month before the removal of the halo, Jane was sent home to continue recuperation. In order for me to continue my work, Jane was provided with 12 hours of nursing care daily on Monday through Friday, and eight hours each on Saturday and Sunday. Jane also received physical therapy, occupational therapy, and swallowing therapy to assist her recovery. She continued on her daily TPN, received a daily IV antifungal agent, and was given IV dilaudid with a TPA pump to help relieve her pain. At night, she rested holding my hand or with her head on my shoulder. From this time forward, we always used handicapped parking for her when she was in the car.

Upon leaving the hospital and under doctor's orders, an external service company provided her with a TPA pump and the narcotic for pain. This pump was the size of a small purse and was attached by IV line to one of the Hickman central line catheters. Wherever Jane went, the TPA pump and line went with her. The TPA pump provided a measured dose of dilaudid, a strong intravenous pain medicine, which she required for much of the rest of her life. Monthly visits to the pain clinic to monitor, oversee, and write orders for this treatment were necessary. For the rest of her life, pain clinic doctors made a real difference in pain management and her opportunity to live normally with her pain under control. Occasionally, the doctor ordered the rate or dosage changed, as was necessary to allow her to live with her pain. When the nurses were not on duty, I provided the nursing procedures to manage this equipment. During her most recent hospital stay, she had become an invalid and used handicapped parking from this time on. She used a wheelchair for most movement and for sitting, and a walker for moving short distances around the house.

Due to the heavy weight of the halo, Jane was unable to lift herself up from bed and required constant and close attention. The home nurses planned her naps when they wrote their notes. They were able to support Jane's strong will and desire to get better. We tried a hospital bed at home, but she preferred her own bed. She worked hard with the therapists and nurses, and gradually improved. She used a walker to move throughout the house. Her bathroom needs were taken care of by a commode, which was placed next to the bed. She had a good time with the nurses, and they laughed and joked a great deal. I fed Jane breakfast and the nurses cleaned up the dishes. At lunch, the nurses prepared a meal. For dinner, Jane and the nurses prepared the meal together. Sometimes the nurses ate with us, and I did the dishes after they had left. Jane was always happy and optimistic, even under the worst situations.

One month after beginning home care, the day nurse, Donna, and I took Jane in my car to the hospital to have her halo removed. It was with great difficulty that Jane maneuvered her neck and head into the car for this trip to the hospital, while the halo was still on. We were all very apprehensive when the halo was removed to see if the bones had fused prop-

                                    Calvin Keeler, Sr.

erly. Everyone, including the doctor and particularly Jane, was ecstatic when the results were perfect and Jane returned home.

From this point on, she was able to enjoy the company of the nurses more. Jane and the evening nurse would laugh themselves silly when she put dishes and silverware into in a little cloth bag that they had attached to the walker, and she went back and forth about the kitchen setting up the dinner table. She made a difficult time pleasant.

From April to mid-September of 1996, Jane continued to have severe pain in her spinal cord. It was so severe that she entered the hospital three more times in April, June, and August for treatment. Each time an MRI was done, and each time more neurosurgeries removed fungal abscesses from different areas of the thoracic and lumbar spine. And, each time she spent a few days in the neurosurgical ICU on a breathing respirator. Even at this point after the August surgery, there were still some hot spots. She was home for one month each before the admittances in April, June, and August. On September 15, 1996, the neurosurgeons decided not to do any more spinal surgeries, as they were getting more difficult and there was little progress to show. Further, the risk was increasing that she might become severely incapacitated or even have her life threatened by surgery. There had been substantial spinal deterioration, and there were many spinal changes as a result. They believed that it was irresponsible and unproductive to continue with more spinal neurosurgeries.

Jane was sent home on comfort or hospice care only. Fortunately for her, comfort care did not mean withdrawal of all procedures and care, but only meant that there would be no more spinal surgeries and that she would be given enough pain medicine to keep her comfortable until the end. We were able to have the physical and other therapies continued along with her TPN, the IV antifungal treatments, and the IV dilaudid with the TPA. They expected her to have more spinal abscesses and to be returned to the hospital shortly when the pain became too great to remain home, just to provide her with ever-increasing amounts of pain medicine as she became paralyzed. They did not expect her to survive very long.

At home, I soon realized that Jane had a great determination to live, and that although Jane had several painful areas in her spine, they were not getting any worse. The nurses and I had several very heated disagreements as I titrated down the IV pain medication in the evening, while they were trying to follow orders to increase the pain medication to provide comfort during the day. Jane fooled almost everyone and won. In the evening and nighttime, with reduced medicine, she became more lucid and alert, and enjoyed more activities. Gradually the pain became more tolerable, and the IV dilaudid was finally terminated many months later. Unfortunately, the IV dilaudid was reinstated as required for normal living with pain a couple of years later when she contracted aspergillosis. She had survived this ordeal and death

    Calvin Keeler, Sr.

sentence, just as she had done many times before. Although her spine still had severe pain and required heavy pain medication, there were no more requirements for neurosurgical intervention.

The years 1997 through 1999 were good years. Jane used her wheelchair when she went out with me. She could also walk around the house and elsewhere by holding my hand. We went to church, restaurants, grocery shopping, and the mall. She went everywhere with the wheelchair and did not let that stop her from living a full life. Our boating days had ended in 1995, as that would have been much too difficult for her to do after all that had transpired. At night, she was on TPN, and from time to time, I gave her IV antibiotics as prescribed. Pain was handled by oral medications.

In 1996, she developed a bleeding esophageal ulcer, probably due to the oral potassium supplements that she had been taking and also due to the analgesics Bufferin and Tylenol, of which she had taken very large quantities for years to manage her pain. It is now well known that these analgesics may have a very destructive effect on the lining of the stomach and the duodenum. An endoscopy showed a malformed stomach with many large folds. These folds also delayed the emptying of the stomach contents into the duodenum. Treatment consisted of multiple hospital admissions, endoscopies, blood transfusions, and a further modification of her diet. By April 1998, the bleeding had stopped, but only after dozens of units of transfusions.

Learning from Jane

In March 1997, Jane's mother, who was 95 and was living with Jane's sister Eileen, began to deteriorate rapidly. I took Jane by car to see her in Connecticut. Her mother was overjoyed to see her, and Jane sat quietly holding her hands for some time. Upon returning home, we learned that her mother had died within an hour after we had left. It appears that her mother was waiting to see her daughter one last time. Jane stood the trip reasonably well, but we would not make any other quick trips outside of the local area. I officiated at the funeral of Jane's mother. Calvin and our grandson Timothy came from Delaware to sing and show their respect, but Jane was unable to make the trip to Connecticut for the funeral service.

Also, in January 1997, my father was diagnosed with cancer of the colon. He had an operation which accomplished very little, and died the following August. Since Jane still had nursing care, I was able to visit him from time to time in the spring and summer. I conducted the funeral service for my father in August in Connecticut. My sister took care of the rest of the arrangements, including the luncheon afterwards. Our son came from Delaware to be with me and to show his respect for his grandfather, but Jane was unable to make the trip from Massachusetts.

In March 1997, I retired from full-time work and was able to spend my full days with Jane. Nurses were withdrawn in September of that year. We had a good year from a recuperative perspective. Although we had conquered the fungus candida, Jane's immune system continued to be compromised, as will be shortly evident.

In June 1997, Calvin's wife, Sharon, earned her Ph.D. in microbiology at the university. We were very sorry that we were not able to travel to attend that celebration. Since then, she has worked as a senior research scientist at a large local corporation.

In the spring of 1998, Jane had basal cell carcinoma of her right leg and of the right side of her nose. The cancers were removed. The surgery on the right side of the nose left a hole right down to her nostril. That required the reconstruction of her nose, taking a piece of tissue from her ear lobe. She also got staph epi from the removal of one growth, which we successfully treated with IV antibiotics.

In 1998, except for her basal cell carcinoma, her life was looking up, and she was enjoying each and every day. I cannot over emphasize enough her will power and ability to lead a full life. Her diet and general physical condition were stable. Her regular checkups with the doctor were routine. She was still on TPN, and her blood tests were consistently stable. Pain was not an overwhelming issue, and was controlled with oral medication. Life seemed to have entered a quiet and rewarding stretch, where we spent our days together. We were very happy, and looked forward to visits from our children and grandchildren.

Chapter 9

Triumph in the Final Years

1999 - 2002

In early 1999, it appeared that Jane was doing much better since her pancreatitis issues had been resolved, her spinal surgeries and other treatments had prevented the spread of her fungal disease, her esophageal bleeding had been stopped, the TPN was sufficient along with a reasonable diet, and the basal cell carcinoma issues had been corrected. It seemed to us that Jane was becoming more stable and was able to look forward to several more happy years together with me during our retirement. Little did I realize that I was unconsciously watching the continuing damage to her immune system, as became apparent over the next three years. In the end, her immune system was severely impaired and unable to stop further infections.

In January, I noticed that she was weaker, and it was becoming more difficult for her to climb the five steps of our split entry ranch from the front door to the main floor, even with my assistance. I also understood that the cost of maintaining this large house, along with high property taxes, was sapping our retirement funds. I therefore proposed that we sell the large house of nine rooms and three bathrooms and move to a smaller one-floor ranch that would be easier for her. I further proposed that we search for such a house in the Boston suburbs. After a couple of days of discussion, she said that she agreed with the decision to move, but that if we were to move, we should move to Delaware so that "you would be near our son and family after I am gone."

This was one of those times when her wisdom greatly exceeded my reasoning and understanding. There were times in the last several years when I have observed that her wisdom was way out in front of me, and I have come to realize and to value how important those times were. She wanted to be certain that I was moved and comfortably settled near our family before her next and possibly final series of crises.

It took over one month for the truth and reality of her statement to sink in on me. During that month, we held several quiet discussions about where we should move. She was insistent and unwilling to change. By way of a rationalization for the move, I concluded that whenever she did get sick, I could drive her back to her doctors at the Massachusetts

                                              Calvin Keeler, Sr.

General Hospital. I therefore, reluctantly agreed to move to Delaware and away from the close contact with our doctors in the Boston area. Many decisions are compromises, and this was one of those. I was not happy with the compromise, but knew that we could not stay in that particular house. We had to do something. The doctors were agreeable, although skeptical. I will admit that over the next few months until we moved, I had many days of serious misgivings about our move to Delaware and wished that I could find another way. I did follow through in future years on returning her to the Massachusetts hospital when she did get sicker, but I unfortunately permitted her to delay some of the trips longer than I should have allowed.

We placed our home in Lexington on the market and in March signed a contract for sale for delivery in August. We received a fair price. After the conclusion of our contract for the sale of the home, I signed a contract with a developer in Delaware to build a house there. Our son sent us plans and other information so I could select a lot with a large backyard, and so that I could select the appropriately sized six-room ranch. I modified the plans to include a ramp for the front sidewalk to the front door without stairs, to raise the level of the back porch so that the step-down was only a couple of inches, and to change other doors and fixtures to make it more convenient for an invalid. Our son was instrumental in this endeavor and made many visits to the house as it was being constructed. The house was completed perfectly, except that it was not delivered in August as we requested, but rather in October 1999.

There were three issues in the timeframe of May to August 1999 that were a cause for concern about our impending move to Delaware. Unfortunately, we had already taken several legal steps towards the move that would have been difficult to reverse, and I hoped that my back up plan of travel to the MGH would be sufficient. First, in June an MOH procedure was successfully used to remove a squamus cell carcinoma from the right leg. Secondly, in July there was a repair of a deviated septum that went well. Thirdly and most importantly, in the May to July timeframe, she began to have moderate pain of a continuous nature in her left face and cheek. This was even more ominous than we realized. An MRI was taken in July, and the results were negative, showing no cause. Thus, since all three issues appeared to be satisfactorily resolved, we proceeded with our plans to move.

I required hospitalization in the spring for a few days due to an infection in my right wrist. Therefore, I did not have the energy to begin to plan the move until early summer. I hired a small dumpster so that we could dispose of many old boxes of work records, a broken lawnmower, two broken bicycles, and other junk that had accumulated over a period of thirty-six years. I was able to picture the new house plans in my mind as to how we would place our furniture, and therefore Jane and I gave the furniture that we could not use to close friends and several members of our family. The furniture that we gave away included a twin bedroom set, a couch, pictures, and several chairs.

By the end of July and early August, the sorting and planning had begun in earnest, and our son arrived with his van to help us. His help in planning, packing, and transporting the items we needed on an interim basis in his van was highly appreciated and made the difference between success and failure. He worked very hard. On the seventh of August, the moving company packed all of the rest of our furnishings and clothing for the trip.

For the night on the day of the move from Lexington, we stayed in a motel in the western suburbs of the Boston area. The next day we drove all the way to Delaware with just a couple of short stops. Jane did not complain about her pains, and the left facial pain was not yet severe. Although she was very tired, she stood the trip well, and we arrived safely. We took with us the equipment and supplies for the TPN that I administered to Jane nightly. We also carefully carried our glucose monitoring and insulin supplies. Within a couple of weeks, we had transferred the TPN infusion preparation to a local company and were using a local doctor for the TPN orders.

The moving company placed our furnishings in storage in Delaware, since our new home was not ready. Calvin and Sharon graciously offered us the use of their master bedroom in their home for two months while our house was being finished.

Fortunately, we had taken with us the things we might need for an interim period.

In August, Jane and I visited the homebuilder several times and selected the carpeting, the kitchen flooring, and the countertops in the bathrooms and the kitchen. The decisions that Jane made resulted in a very attractive home for us when it was completed.

Calvin and Sharon took very good care of us while we stayed with them. On Friday, October 13, 1999, we moved into our new home. We directed the movers where to place the furniture and directed the unpacking of several boxes. We felt well enough organized to move into our own home that night and were able to give Calvin and Sharon back their master bedroom. Over the next couple of weeks, we unpacked most of the boxes, hung pictures, and placed things in the proper locations throughout the house. The move went well, and the furniture fit the rooms almost exactly as we had planned. Calvin and Sharon helped us unpack several boxes and place our linens and dishes in the right places. Quickly, with her good sense of color and propriety, Jane purchased curtains and draperies. She knew exactly what she wanted, and they finished off the house very nicely. Thus, our new home in Delaware became her refuge.

I have never ceased to be amazed by her courage and bravery for moving so far from her doctors in Boston and for moving into our new house in Delaware with all new surroundings and contacts. For someone so ill for so long, this is a remarkable

     Calvin Keeler, Sr.

testament to her faith and her courage. She was a very strong person.

By early November, Jane had run out of energy and was unable to do any more serious work in unpacking and setting up the house. We had only a dozen or so large, less important boxes left to unpack, and so we delayed further unpacking until she felt better. In late fall and early winter I took her grocery shopping in a wheelchair, and we visited several doctors to establish new relationships in our new community.

Jane's best friend, Jean, in Lexington honored and pleased Jane when she reported to her what she had done. On "All Saint's Sunday" in November, she had taken Jane's picture to church as her "saint." Jane's courage and faith had touched her deeply. When Jane's friend and I talked recently, she said that she still honors Jane's memory. On Christmas Eve, I took Jane to our new church in Delaware in her wheelchair for services. Going places and doing things were getting more difficult for her.

By mid-December, we had the local doctors in Delaware involved in trying to determine why Jane's left face and cheek hurt so badly. X-rays were inconclusive. By mid-January 2000, we started a six-week course of IV antibiotics, which I administered at home. By the end of February, it was clear that the pains were significantly worse, the IV antibiotics had not helped, and something else needed to be done.

During February, I urged Jane to let me take her back to the doctors who knew her the best at the research center of the Massachusetts General Hospital in Boston. She declined, fearing that the trip would be too exhausting, and feeling that her problems were not that ominous. She knew how to live with pain and wanted to stay in her new home in Delaware. However, this was the beginning of the next to last stage of the complete breakdown of her immune system. I had then and still have no way of knowing that her life would have been any different had we made the trip, although I do now wish that I had been more insistent and tried.

Before the increasing pain and illness further prevented her, I was able to take her to church for another time in early March so we could transfer our church membership from the Lexington church to the Ebenezer United Methodist Church in Newark, Delaware.

The pain in Jane's left face contin-ued to increase and reached severe proportions. Concurrently, the pain medicine was unable to improve her ability to live normally. Therefore, just before mid-March, 2000, she was seen by a local ENT (Ear, Nose, and Throat) specialist. On May 18, the ENT specialist performed a left endoscopic sinusotomy at Wilmington Hospital, a part of the Christiana Hospital complex. Jane always recovered very quickly from minor surgeries, and thus she was permitted to return home about twelve hours after the surgery. For the next month and a half, we saw the ENT specialist every week. During this period, Jane's pain continued to worsen, and the doctor was unable

          Calvin Keeler, Sr.

to understand why the surgery had not resolved the problem. She was being treated with a variety of sinus care medicines, but the proper follow-up with pathology was not done.

On the weekend of April 29, 2000, her left facial pains got substantially worse, her left eye swelled up, and it became totally blind. We had an emergency meeting with the primary care doctor, and a retina specialist ophthalmologist saw her. She was admitted to the Christiana Hospital, a large, very qualified acute care level Delaware hospital. She received an MRI, CT scans, and many other tests. The diagnosis made by the doctors in this admission was perfectly correct: that she had an aspergillus fungus from her left sinuses to her left eye, to the left optic nerve, to the left orbit, and to the base of the skull. This was a virulent form of fungus, and except for still unpublished unusual research procedures, there was absolutely no known treatment for it. At that time, there were no medicines available which could penetrate the brain barrier to stop this fungus. She was diagnosed with aspergillosis of the brain and was totally blind in her left eye. The doctors admitted that this was a death sentence, and they sent us by ambulance on Sunday to Jefferson University Hospital, a research hospital in Philadelphia.

At Jefferson University Hospital, a top neurosurgeon pulled together a team of surgeons in several specialties and proposed a solution. In addition to a massive invasive sinusotomy, they wanted to remove the top of her skull, move the brain to one side, and scrape inside the skull cavity to remove the fungus. We were both in shock. I spent the entire night awake, in meditation and in prayer. By morning, I knew my answer, and I would have held to that answer no matter who might disagree. Fortunately, Jane also thought about it and had independently come to the same conclusion that the prognosis for that suggested operation was poor and that we would not proceed. She and I did not wish her to become a vegetable with a life expectancy of a month or so and with such a remote chance for recovery. Our son came and picked us up, and we left the hospital and returned to our home in Delaware, where we once again contacted the doctors that were caring for Jane there and informed them of our decision.

I was very sad about the prospects of losing my dearest love and displayed a few tears in the doctor's office. The doctor prescribed an anti-depressant for me. The pills made me feel strange, so I stopped taking them, which did not please the doctor. I am convinced that it is acceptable and necessary to feel sad when the situation is this grave, and the medical establishment does us an injustice when doctors try to insulate us from these very proper and necessary feelings. Grieving is a part of restoration and renewal.

From May through August of 2000, Jane was placed on hospice care in order to provide as much comfort as possible. We made frequent trips to the pain clinic where they repeatedly increased the dosage of the IV pain medicine. However, the pain con-

Calvin Keeler, Sr.

tinued to worsen to the point where it was almost unbearable day and night. There was no relief. Jane was given a large quantity of steroids to reduce inflammation, which also resulted in some side effects. She was still on her nightly TPN, and I could see no other symptoms of failing life systems except for the intolerable pain. The only plan that we or the doctors had was to wait for her to die.

It was during this period that the church to which we had recently transferred our membership (the Ebenezer United Methodist Church in Newark, Delaware) assigned Douglas Kellogg, a Stephen's minister, to visit and help us. A Stephen's minister is a lay member who is given training to assist others who might be facing a crisis, such as terminal illness, family life crisis, divorce, or some other major faith-challenging event. The man assigned to us visited us every week except for those weeks while we were in the Massachusetts General Hospital in Boston. I appreciated his visits, discussions, and prayers, while Jane appreciated his singing some old gospel hymns to her. We always looked forward to his visits, be they at home when Jane was home or in the hospital. This man has remained my very close friend ever since.

On a Sunday in the first half of August 2000, Jane made her last trip to the church in Delaware for worship services. We went by car, and she used her wheelchair with her limited mobility and limited walking abilities. Her left eye was blind and slightly swollen, but she sat erect. She was unable to remain until the conclusion of the service. For all of her life, she had enjoyed going to church on every Sunday to worship. After this service, she was never again strong enough or well enough to go to church.

Since we were making no progress towards Jane's recovery and were just waiting for her to die, in mid-August I gathered the several MRI's and other tests that had been taken in Delaware, put them in a package, and used overnight FedEx to send them to Dr. Godine at the Massachusetts General Hospital in Boston. He was on vacation, but during his vacation time, he took the MRI's to several specialists at the MGH and other qualified physicians whom he knew. We were overjoyed when he called to say that they thought they could help Jane. He had never let us down.

On August 24, 2000, I chartered a two-engine air ambulance with a nurse and a pilot and took her from a local airport, New Castle County Airport, to Logan Airport and the MGH in Boston. I am still amazed at her trust in me and my decision when she was so weak, to take a small plane into such unknowns. At an affiliated hospital, the Massachusetts Eye and Ear Clinic, located next door and attached to the MGH, an ENT surgeon who had been using some experimental drugs on aspergillosis patients performed surgery. He performed a biopsy and an exteneration of the left orbit back to the base of skull. In other words, he removed her left eye in total. The surgery took about two hours, and at first,

                    Calvin Keeler, Sr.

she seemed to stand it well. The resulting biopsy completely confirmed the diagnosis of the fungus.

The aspergillosis disease was treated first with Amphotericin Lipid complex and then with an investigational IV drug named Voriconazole after the aspergillus had penetrated the dura. We daily filled her left eye socket with an amphotericin-saturated gauze for a few months. After the successful eradication of the fungus aspergillus, I treated her left eye with gauze pads saturated with saline solution for the rest of her life. The treatment to place a prosthesis in the left eye socket would have taken several hours of major surgery, and she was never again strong enough for that.

Although her left eye had been removed and her right eye had complete macular degeneration, she still saw peripherally in her right eye. She compensated so well and tried so hard, that she acknowledged whatever she was shown, looked at people when they talked with her, and managed to actually see a great deal, and even to eat without problems. A couple of times she said to me, "Be careful with the gauze so as not to hurt my eye." Until the final few days, she willed herself to make do and compensate with partial sight in one eye. I was amazed at her courage and ability day after day. Her life near the end was one long story of pain and suffering, lived with grace. She lived and endured right up to the end with dignity and faith.

The innovative surgery and procedures, and the use of the investigational drugs did cure her of her aspergillus fungus. However, the damage to her immune system had been done, and the side effects of the use of steroids are well known. After recovery, she went back to her room at the MGH. Within three days, she "coded." Her lungs were overwhelmed with pneumonia, and the recovery team rushed to her room to intubate her. She was taken to the Medical ICU and placed on a breathing ventilator. This was a very difficult time for her in the ICU and lasted for two months. She had sepsis (staph aureus) and klebsiella pneumonia. She was intubated from September 1st until September 22nd, when a more permanent tracheotomy was performed. The tracheotomy was removed four months later on January 22nd, 2001.

While in the ICU, she was treated with IV antibiotics and IV antifungal medicines. She was sedated for the entire ICU stay of two months. About half way into her confinement in the ICU, her chemistries deteriorated badly, and the ICU staff took me to a private conference room and told me that they did not believe that she would survive more than a day or so. I would not approve of an order for non-resuscitation. Dr. Godine had seen her recover previously from severe illnesses and therefore maintained a high level of medical care. She survived one heart block in this ICU stay and recovered. The intubation resulted in a delayed swallowing reflex, as often occurs from such elongated medical emergencies. This condition stayed with her and worsened severely towards the end. From this point on, she only drank thickened liquids and was required to make a conscious effort to swallow correctly every time.

During the six-month stay at the MGH, I spent every day and night with Jane in the hospital room, except that I was not able to stay with her overnight when she was in the ICU. Therefore, on the first night that she was in the ICU, I went to the gift shop and bought her an ultra light stuffed lamb. I figured that if a newborn infant might grasp a light cuddle thing of a couple of ounces, then perhaps Jane could hold onto it. She did, and the nurses always put the lamb under her left hand while she was resting. Even while she was sedated, she knew that it was there and held onto it. It was a reminder that I would return when she had finished resting. I was very satisfied with the symbol, and she grew very attached to it during her many stays in ICU's over the next two years.

In this and all subsequent confinements in the Medical ICU, both at the MGH and in Delaware, I usually sat quietly by her, holding her hand and talking gently with her. It is unusual for a member of the family to be allowed to spend so much time with a patient in the ICU, but it was apparent to all that she was responding well to my close attention. At the MGH, I normally spent from 6 A.M. to 9 P.M. with her daily, except for when the nurses, doctors, and staff were working with her. I am convinced that their permission for my attendance along with the light stuffed lamb were instrumental in her retaining her cognition and alertness when they aroused her from the sedation at the end of the stay.

During this same admission of six months at the MGH, she had two more visits to the Medical ICU, once for another code for severe pneumonia and respiratory failure and once for a duodenal ulcer bleed out. She had one more heart block in the ICU, which was resolved without surgical intervention. This was a long admission for her, but she grew stronger and stronger, and on January 25, 2001, I chartered another two-engine air ambulance with a nurse and a pilot to fly home to Delaware.

The day after we arrived home, the local primary care physician, internist Dr. Stephanie Ciccarelli, came to our house to see for herself how Jane was doing. The doctor was amazed that Jane was sitting in her wheelchair at the kitchen table and was alert and cogent. Jane spent a little over one month enjoying our home, grandchildren, and family. Home nursing, physical therapy, occupational therapy, and swallowing therapy were restarted. She continued with her nightly TPN and continuous dilaudid infusion via a TPA pump.

After about a month, I noticed that Jane was beginning to show symptoms of pneumonia once more. In her case, the threat of pneumonia never left her until she died a little over one year later. First, whenever anyone is afflicted with a swallowing reflex problem, it is very easy to aspirate saliva into the lungs and to reinitiate pneumonia. Secondly, having complete respiratory failure, which in Jane's case required three visits to the ICU in her previous hospitalization, usually results in a permanent weakening of the lungs and a susceptibility to many future and opportunistic infections of the lungs.

On February 28, 2001, I drove Jane to the MGH in Boston. She stood the trip well and was admitted for treatment of pneumonia. A few days later while in the hospital, her breathing became extremely difficult and a "code" was called. When the emergency team got to her room, she was not breathing and they could find no pulse in her wrists and ankles. Her heart was barely beating. The doctor turned to me and said, "Should we stop treatment?" Frequent respiratory failures, such as hers, do not respond well to treatment. I replied that we had not yet come to agreement to do that and that we should proceed. They proceeded to intubate Jane and performed external heart massage to restart her heart. As always with Jane, her body responded well and she recovered from very brink of death. They took her to the Medical ICU, were she stayed for a little more than a month.

When she had improved, had left the ICU, and was recovering in her room, I explained to her what a "near-death experience" is and asked her if she had had one. She replied that she had not. About three months later, I explained to her how truly close to death that she had been. Her response to me was, "Thank you for saving my life." Once more, she confirmed that I was making the decisions that she wanted me to make when she was not able to make them herself. She recovered quickly from the pneumonia and remained in the hospital for a little less than six weeks. Upon discharge, we drove home again without incident to Delaware.

From mid-March until the end of June in 2001, Jane had four admissions to the Christiana Hospital only a few miles from our home in Delaware. From this time on, except for the two remaining car trips to the MGH in Boston, whenever Jane needed to go to or from the hospital, the usual method was by ambulance. Each of these four admissions was only for a week or two, although some required intubations (once in the ER upon arrival) and intensive care due to the infections of the lung and bronchial system, such as staph, VRE, Klebsiella, and other organisms. Treatment always meant the use of IV antibiotics.

From July 1st through the end of August, Jane spent two months at home, enjoying her grandchildren and family and enjoying short trips to the grocery store. Even at this advanced stage of her disease, and although respiratory failure was a constant companion, she enjoyed every day of her life and looked forward to each new morning. She was grateful for each day of her life. Home nursing, physical therapy, occupational therapy, and swallowing therapy were restarted.

She always enjoyed eating her food, both at home and in the hospital. At home, every breakfast consisted of a poached egg on toast, coffee, and juice. She ate very carefully, usually with thickening in the liquids. She always bowed her head in prayer to thank her creator. Sometimes in the hospital, it was heartbreaking to watch her giving thanks for clear broth or some other restricted diet meal, but it was important to her.

At 5 A.M. on the Friday before Labor Day in 2001, I heard Jane choke and aspirate while sleeping. I knew that that meant another round of pneumonia, and so our son and I drove all night to take her to the MGH in Boston. This admission did not require intubation or a stay in the ICU. It was treated with IV antibiotics. An MRI was taken for comparison of the aspergillosis of the brain and to determine if there were any other brain changes occurring. The MRI showed no change in six months, and therefore it was believed that the fungus had been stopped and the investigational drug voriconazole was discontinued.

Heavy use of steroids and heavy use of pain medicines had been causing an altered mental status from time to time. Nothing was found, and therefore there was no change in treatment. Her altered mental status occurred infrequently and was of minor duration. We drove home on September 11 and 12, staying with her sister Eileen in Connecticut overnight on the 11th, the day of the terrorist attack on the twin towers in New York, since New York was impassible. On September 12th, we drove across the Hudson River on the Tappan Zee Bridge without incident. As we traveled south on the Garden State Parkway in New Jersey, we could see to the east a huge cloud of smoke rising from southern Manhattan where the twin towers had stood. It was a fearful and overwhelming sight.

In October, I drove Jane to the MGH for

another admission of fourteen days for pneumonia and mucus secretions. Treatment resolved the symptoms, and we drove home without incident.

In November, Jane spent five days in the Christiana Hospital for a GI bleed from a duodenal ulcer. After an endoscopy for diagnosis, the ulcer resolved on its own, but she needed eight units of blood transfused. She was also treated for continuing pneumonia. In late November and early December, she spent ten days at the Christiana Hospital for a tibia fracture. She had fallen at home while attempting to use the commode. A breakage of bones is a common setback to seriously ill patients, and I knew the implications. The fracture was set with a cast, which bothered her considerably, since she was having contracture of that leg. Three months later, the hard cast was replaced with a soft cast, but the fracture never set and healed. Again, she was treated for continuing pneumonia. At this point, she went NPO and discontinued all pills, resulting in reducing the mucous and improving the pneumonia symptoms slightly. This was the very last time that she ate or took anything by mouth.

However, too much damage had been done to the pulmonary system and to her swallowing reflex by all of the intubations and illnesses. Thus, in late December I heard her once again aspirate saliva. This resulted in severe pneumonia and a prolonged stay in the Christiana Hospital through her death in June 2002, except for a few days in March and a few days in early June. Throughout the entire period, she had

Calvin Keeler, Sr.

problems with her lungs, and her pneumonia infiltrate persisted.

The damage to Jane's immune system was by now almost complete, and it was fully compromised. From this time on, she was the object of many opportunistic infections, which required constant treatment and frequent changes in her antibiotics. However, we did not observe any further fungal infections.

Dr. Stephanie Ciccarelli (Internist) and Dr. Mark Zubrow (Director of Medical Intensive Care) led a team of physicians and medical support staff at the Christiana Hospital in an heroic effort for quality of life for Jane during her last six months of life. Every possible treatment available to a large trauma and acute care hospital was used. Jane amazed everyone, including the medical staff, at her courage, her will to live, and her ability to survive.

Shortly after this admission to the Christiana Hospital and just before Christmas 2001, she developed severe breathing problems and advanced pneumonia again. She "coded," and they called the emergency team to respond. She was intubated and placed in the Medical ICU. She remained there for sixty days for a difficult recovery and was under sedation for the entire time. She required heavy doses of IV antibiotics, and for the particular infection that was most prevalent in her lungs, she required an antibiotic that damaged her kidneys. Up until this point, her kidneys had always been strong enough to overcome the effects of the antibiotics and the medicines that she had received. But now, the damage was too severe and there was renal failure as the kidneys shut down. The medical team asked me if she would want to be put on kidney dialysis for the rest of her life, or if we should just let her go.

The recuperative powers of her body were amazing for her entire medical journey. For all of the dozens of major surgeries, some with incisions of more than twelve inches, she healed quickly with minimal scarring for the size of the incisions. There were times when I could not understand how her body could heal such massive incisions, but it always did. Sometimes the incisions were so massive that the healing took weeks and required extensive home care after discharge from the hospital. Similarly for all of her medicines and drugs given to her, her liver and kidneys had always recovered. At times, they were under stress, but they never failed to recover up until this last insult. There were instances where I do not understand how they absorbed such quantities of drugs, some with extensive toxic side effects. Perhaps the reasons for this were her unshakable faith in her Lord, her very healthy attitude about life, and her good eating habits that she enjoyed all her life of natural, wholesome, unprocessed foods.

I thought about kidney dialysis for a few days, hoping that her kidneys might recover once more on their own. When they did not, much to the dismay of the medical team and my family, I elected to start her on kidney dialysis. They had all considered that she was too sick to recover and felt that it would be better if we just let her pass. As her legal spokesperson, I felt that I must always be very faithful to her wishes, and that my decisions must be the ones that she would have made. She had always agreed and confirmed my decisions when she had recovered from sedation, and she once again concurred when awakened almost two months later. The medical team relented under my firm request, and started her on kidney dialysis. They needed to place a permanent dialysis catheter in her. A couple of weeks later, her kidneys appeared to begin to function again due to output and creatinine level improvements, and I was hopeful that her kidneys might recover. But then she received another insult of infection and antibiotics, which shut down her kidneys for good. She was on kidney dialysis for the rest of her life.

After twenty-one days, her intubation was replaced with a tracheotomy. This tracheotomy was maintained in her throat for the rest of her life. She had several more admissions to the Medical ICU during these last six months, and they used the tracheotomy each time.

Not only doctors, but also some extended family members complained that I was prolonging her life and suffering unnecessarily. I was very certain of her wishes and did not deviate, but remained true to her requests to me. She always felt that life was a precious gift and not be wasted or relinquished voluntarily. She enjoyed her time on earth, even when she was unable to do the things that she wanted to do. Frequently doctors see patients who want to leave this world when they can no longer function.

However, Jane was mostly alert and cogent, and our time together was comforting and precious to both of us.

In mid-March she appeared fairly stable, and we both requested that she be allowed to go home. At home, we restarted our home nursing services, including her TPN and her IV pain medicine. About six days later, her blood glucose level dropped precipitously. I needed to give her a bolus D50W ampule of glucose intravenously. Occasionally, I had been provided with such ampules to administer, but this time I did not have one. Due to her swallowing issues, I could not give her sugar by mouth. Therefore, I needed to take her back to the ER at the hospital to save her from glucose shock and death. They examined, admitted, and unfortunately kept her.

For the next three months, she was placed on a portable breathing ventilator in her regular hospital private room, using the tracheotomy during her sleep periods at night. She absolutely hated the tracheotomy and the ventilator, and she occasionally tried to remove them since they felt so abnormal. She wanted to live, but in a half-sleep stage at night, she required close watching. I stayed with her all night each night, and occasionally I could hear her fumbling at the devices. Then I would hold her hand.

Her last three months were subject to the many problems of an overwhelming illness. She had regular treatments of kidney dialysis, and required a large amount of IV antibiotics and other medicines. A couple of weeks into this last admission, she had another serious bout of pneumonia and coded. The Medical ICU doctor asked her whether she wanted to go back to the ICU with sedation or tough it out in her room with the antibiotics. She had had enough of the ICU, thought that she could lick the pneumonia, and chose to remain in her room. She successfully fought through this case of pneumonia.

A few weeks later, she said to me, "My life isn't worth much, but I enjoy living and living is better than not living." Life was still worth it for her, and I knew that she still enjoyed being with me. She was always grateful for each day. I agreed that life was valuable and told her that I loved her very much. She was always exceedingly humble and never thought of herself as important.

For the preceding year, there were many bouts of extreme and debilitating illness. It should be no surprise then that there were times of mental confusion as to where she was, and even as to which hospital. Some of this was a natural consequence of having been sedated in the ICU for such long periods over the preceding two years. Additionally, she was occasionally sedated to keep her quiet during lengthy MRI procedures, once with general anesthesia. There were also times when some medicines had an hallucinogenic effect, as well as times when the medicines caused angry and aggressive reactions in her. Some medicines had extremely negative side effects. Sometimes when she was extremely weak, there might be paranoid symptoms during which she believed that the hospital or me or others were keeping her from getting well. None of this is unusual for this level of illness. During her last year, most such episodes lasted for a couple of days at most. She always knew me, and she always knew our son and family. It is a testament to her strong willpower that she fought through each time of confusion and lack of clarity to become fully cogent and normal. Many doctors and nurses expressed from time to time their absolute amazement at her strength and willpower. She touched many lives, and she left a lasting imprint on them for what is possible in life. She never let the cobwebs cloud her mind for long.

About a month before she died, her primary care doctor came in and said, "You know you're very sick and are going to go to heaven soon." Jane replied, "Yes I know, and I'm ready to go today, tomorrow, or next week." Then the doctor said, "How do you feel?" Jane replied, "I feel terrible. I hurt, and I just don't feel good." The doctor responded, "What do you want me to do?" The doctor expected an answer that Jane wished to end her suffering. However, what Jane responded was always her reply, "Fix me up and send me home." Outside of the room, the doctor told me that she did not understand, but I understood fully. Jane frequently told me that she was ready at any time to go home to her God, and that she was not afraid, but that for now she just wanted to go home with me.

In May, I asked Jane's former hairdresser, who frequently visited private residences and nursing homes, to come to the hospital to her room and

                                      Calvin Keeler, Sr.

to cut, wash and set her hair. It had not been done for perhaps seven months. Her hairdresser gladly complied, and started the work carefully. About three-quarters done, Jane said that she was too tired to proceed. Therefore, I held her close and supported her in my arms while the hairdresser quickly finished the work. Jane had always seen her hairdresser every week, and I knew that this act of kindness made her feel a whole lot better.

About two weeks before the end, Jane reported to me one morning that she had had a vivid dream of her father and her older sister Lois, both of whom had died many years before. I listened attentively, but did not inquire too deeply into Jane's personal and private dream. This special type of dream is frequently reported as happening to people that are nearing the end in order to prepare them for the passing. I believe that that was the case with Jane. I was somewhat surprised that her mother and her other sister Winifred, both of whom had also died and who had been very close to Jane, did not appear, but the more dominant personalities were the ones that did appear to her.

Over the last year or so, there were times when she seemed highly agitated, and we gave her medicines to calm her down. It is now apparent to me that it was not really agitation as such, but that this was her struggle to overcome her disease, to fight through illness and the cobwebs, to get up, and to get herself well. She was not fighting as such. She always believed that one worked hard to get well, get home, and get on with life. Clearly, she always believed in visualizing her healing and her leaving the hospital better.

About the first of June, she strongly urged and pleaded with me to find a way to get her home. I could see that there was no progress being made in the hospital, and that all we were doing was to prolong life in a diminishing capacity day by day. She just wanted to go home. She believed that she would get better in the comfort of her home. The doctors put up impossible obstructions to our attempts to go home. Therefore, I could see that the only way that we could get permission to go home was for both of us to state that we would go home on hospice care only. If one left the hospital against doctor's orders, there were legal and financial implications involving future hospital admissions and Medicare coverage.

Jane, even at this late date in her medical treatment, had faith that God would help her body to recover to continue a life that she enjoyed, if only she could get home. Each and every day, her primary goal was to get well enough to go home. The miracle of recovery through faith had occurred so many times in her life, that she just expected it to happen again. I had also learned that miracles with her life just continued to happen, and I believed that I should always assist her in what she wanted to do. She did not believe that merely existing in the hospital on a ventilator at night with continuously decreasing and diminishing vitality and life was what our goal for

     Calvin Keeler, Sr.

living should be. She wanted one more chance to really live in this great world.

After we arrived home, we tried to get her back on TPN and kidney dialysis. Hospice said that they would not cover us if we requested this kind of care. This was a complete shock to us, since we had twice before left hospitals on hospice care with TPN and other unusual medical interventions. Further, the doctors were absolutely furious with me, but Jane and I did not want to end her life in a matter of hours. Within two days, her blood glucose levels dropped suddenly, and I took her to the ER, so that they could give her a bolus of glucose. Neither she nor I were ready for her to die so quickly at home. She did not expect me to let her die within one day on something as basic as glucose shock. I just had to give her a chance, and I did. I was also able to obtain another kidney dialysis treatment for her, although with some discomfort by the nephrology team. Being home with full care except for the breathing ventilator at night was the right thing and was something she had to do. She saw her grandchildren and family twice during the four days that she was home. I remember her sitting on the side of her bed and hugging her grandsons, her son, and her daughter-in-law. She never believed in quitting. She just thought that if she got home, she would find a way to get better. Her mind was clear during the days that she was home. These were precious moments.

For most of her time at home, she was lucid and alert. She talked well and visited with hospice, social workers, visiting nurses, and family very intel-ligently, as they questioned our motives. She always had the capacity to reach down and find the strength for normal living. Although she was weak, the strength of her faith and character showed through. She had the faith that she could overcome almost any adversity and recover one more time, as long as she came home. In retrospect, I still believe that this was the right thing to do, and I am glad that we overcame the obstacles to get it done. It was classic Jane. It was one more instance of her ongoing inspiration from being close to our children and grandsons and seeing them so much and experiencing their love during her final three years in Delaware.

About the fourth day and after hospice had declined to assist us, the visiting home nurse came by to begin coverage. Upon examination, it became clear to me and to the nurse that Jane was having dif-ficulty breathing and that her breathing was getting very labored. This was no way to live. I knew that we now had no choice. Therefore, I called the doctor and asked that she be readmitted to the hospital after four days at home and to be put on "comfort care" only. We assured the doctor that our decision was firm and that we would not renege on it. Torture is just not necessary in modern medicine. Being home satisfied Jane and completed something that just had to be done, no matter what. It had also been hard to watch her rest in a standard bed, since she was so weak that she could not keep her head up on the pillow, as it just kept sliding off.

     Calvin Keeler, Sr.

Jane was readmitted to the Christiana Hospital and was placed on medicine that alleviated her labored breathing difficulties. Calvin and Sharon brought the two grandsons in to see her on Thursday, but on the next day Friday, she was too ill to have children as visitors. Thursday night in the middle of the night, I heard noises from her bed, and so I went over to ask what I could do for her. She said that she was praying, so I left her alone and said nothing more at that time, leaving her to her privacy. Her strength came from her faith. She was no stranger to prayer, for she had prayed to God Almighty and sung gospel hymns almost every day of her life, and she had always prayed for guidance in the hospital.

In the last two or three days of her life, her remaining minimal eyesight began to fail completely. She began to say that she could not see, maybe just a very little bit of light. It was excruciatingly sad for me.

On Friday night, she was restless and kept trying to get up. She just knew that she had to will herself up and better. She was feeling herself waning. Every forty-five minutes for most of the night, I kneeled by her bed and, as she sat on the side of the bed, I held her head on my shoulder with my arms tight around her. When she would doze off, I would then pick her up and put her back on her pillow. In about forty-five minutes, she would try to sit up again. Once, she said to me, "I think that I am dying." Through held-back tears, I replied, "You are awful, awful sick." I just could not say any more or in any other way.

On Saturday morning, she was restless, so we quieted her down. I had breakfast and came back to her room. The doctor came in and said that he did not think that she would last the day. Although I knew that she had only a few days to live, I did not believe him yet, since I had watched her rally so many times from death's door before. I now believe that he heard weak heart or weak breath sounds. Calvin came by mid-morning and brought lunch for the two of us. The two of us just sat there together and talked quietly from time to time. She was very quiet. She had always relaxed and treasured the moments when Calvin and I just sat and talked quietly together while she rested. For her entire life, she had always wanted Calvin and me to be together and never ever put herself first. I am sure that at this moment the world felt right to her.

At 1:50 P.M., I said that I did not see her breathing. I went over to her and it appeared that she had gone. Calvin mentioned that her breathing had been erratic and that he had noticed it slowing a little while before. My first thoughts were that she had left her body, that she was gone, and that I would need to hurry if I wanted to have any last words with her. I was not overwhelmed with a feeling of needing to hug her, since she was not there any longer. We called the nurse, who confirmed that she had died. I stood next to the bed and prayed to God for Him to welcome and take care of her and to wipe away her tears. Then I spoke to Jane, and told her that I loved and missed her and to follow the light to heaven where she would find joy and happiness. Her broken body had fallen apart. She had had a strong heart, but now she had failure of her lungs, her kidneys, and her whole body. Her body was now ready to go, as was her soul.

Neither one of us noticed precisely the moment when she died. Her soul knew that it was time, as happens with someone who is really ready, and she died very quietly without any sound at all. She had lived her life the way she had wanted to live, honoring God and life itself until the end, no matter what others might think. She was ready for her Creator, and her life journey was totally completed.

She knew her body well, and for her whole life, she pushed the envelope of her strength in every aspect just as far as she could, until there was none left. Year after year, she had endured pain and struggle, but she ended her long journey in triumph.

I believe that in heaven she heard the angels singing to welcome her.

Sharon arrived in the hospital room just a few minutes later and gave us her support. About an hour later, our local minister, Rev. Ray Graham, arrived for a visit before we had had the time to notify him of her passing. Some things happen because they are supposed to happen.

I supported Jane and worked with her in her illnesses every day for all of our lives together. This was a joint struggle against a major foe. Our deep love and our deep faith sustained us both.

She was a special person, she never complained, and she never said, "Why me?" She never stopped trying, and she never quit. What a glorious witness and what a wonderful journey, in spite of a lifetime of illness and pain. She was a "saint." It is clear that God was very real to her, and that in her meditative and prayer life, He was no stranger to her. She drew her strength from the true Source of life. She was certain that she would see her Risen Lord face to face and not through a glass darkly. She had completely finished the tasks that had been assigned to her for this world. God had truly blessed her life. In reflecting upon the courage and the gifts of her life to those about her, I conclude with two words, "Well done!"

Calvin Keeler, Sr.

Chapter 10

After

Jane and I rarely thought or talked about what would happen to us after we died. We were content to live the best lives that we could in this world with its challenges and without regard for what might come next. We could only make a difference in this life. She enjoyed this life, possessed pleasant thoughts, understood who she was, although she sometimes lacked confidence, and was naturally cheerful and optimistic. No need to worry about what we could not change. We firmly believed that if we lived our lives honestly and prayerfully, we would be in God's hands in this and in the next life, and that it would not matter in what form that next life might occur. She had no expectations or preconceived theories about the nature of heaven, so that should have made her passing somewhat easier. We each firmly believed that God is love, eternal, all-powerful, and has no beginning and no end. All that was necessary was for us was to accept Christ as our savior, and to do our best to permit God's Holy Spirit to guide us.

Almost every day of our many years together was a happy one. We believed that God was very good to us everyday, even when Jane was at her sickest in the hospitals. We wondered why we were so blessed to have such wonderfully happy and rewarding lives, when we had done nothing to deserve them. We were able to enjoy the best living that this world has to offer. Just being together quietly and holding hands, even when she was sick, truly made us feel good.

Jane was very humble at all times and never arrogant. She would never step forward to speak, even though I knew that she could do so ably. She always supported her family and tried to make sure that her husband and her son received proper respect and hearing for our points of view. She always supported and praised my efforts at preaching in church, even when I did not believe it was justified. She would never accept my statements when I told her how unique, or how special and exceptional she was. She was truly gifted in her abilities, in her faith, and in her journey of life. In private discussions with friends, she was careful to be considerate and tolerant of the opinions and ideas of others and not to push her own ideas on others. However, in private with me she would clearly and wisely speak for herself and her feelings. I value all of those memories. She just wanted to live a full and glorious life with her family. She enjoyed every minute of her life, even while ill.

I know that God sent his guardian angels to protect each of us from dangerous situations many times during our lives. I also need to express my gratitude that He sent His guidance to us during times of decisions, and that we were each willing to listen most of the time. The human part of this is that we were not always aware that there was guidance there for us, and thus we sometimes did not hear it.

Since the death of Jane, I have naturally become much more interested in the next life. This was not true for either of us in the losses of our parents. Although my experiences and thoughts are very real to me, I know of no way to apply scientific methodology to validate their authenticity. However, and one should not be surprised, that since I have been willing to meditate and actively listen, phrase questions, and be open to responses, I believe that I have received confirmation that death does not end life. Death releases the human spirit and soul from the body, and life will therefore continue as a soul or energy, to learn and to worship, all without the restrictions of spatial dimensions. It appears that God's plan for our life does not end with death, but only takes on a new and greater meaning, as we enter a new life.

My ability to pierce the veil of the eternal with my vision or reason is nonexistent. Therefore, I cannot describe what the next life will be like.

Since the death of my wife, I have permitted myself to be open to accept input and messages from the beyond. Each of us must make this specific decision, if we want to be attentive to these possibilities. I am convinced that unless we do decide to listen, then we should not be surprised if do not hear very much.

On the day after my wife's funeral, I went to the cemetery to visit her grave. While there, I had the distinct feeling that I received a message that she was OK, that she was happy, and that everything was going to be all right. On the next day, I received a message that we had done all that we could have done, and that in spite of her major illnesses, she had lived to the amazing age of 70 and had enjoyed her whole entire life. I do not believe these messages were just subjective, since they came with such a feeling of her relief and her serenity and her happiness. I had a sense of deep peace and not of emptiness or aloneness.

I have kept a journal of the messages that I believe I have received and refer to it from time to time. In the first two months, the messages seemed more frequent, since I believe that each of us was trying to adjust to this new relationship. In addition, it just seemed so new and unusual that every thought appeared special. I now feel that she watches over me, and that she is involved in everything that I think and do. I feel her happiness when I am happy or having a good experience. Moreover, I feel her encouraging me on the days when I am sad. I know that our love for each other has transcended the veil of death moment by moment.

For the first six months after Jane died, I went to the gravesite almost daily to pray to God and to meditate. I knew that she was not there, but I listened for her. At first, this location assisted me, but then as I became more aware of Jane's constant presence with me, I went to the cemetery less and less. Now I find that I am better able to pray, to meditate, and also to listen to Jane when I am quiet at home or in church.

Many believe that those who have passed to the other side have the ability to influence some parts of nature, such as birds. It is true that for most spring, summer, and fall days when I leave the house or when I arrive home, there is usually at least one bird sitting on the peak of the roof of my house. Rarely do I see birds sitting on the roofs of any other houses in the neighborhood. I choose to believe that this is a message from Jane sending me her love. Sometimes the birds unnaturally fly very near me when I am in the yard, even when I am making loud noises with the power mower. We live near a wild area, and several rabbits seem to gather in our back yard and not in the back yards of my next-door neighbors.

For most of every day, I am aware of her presence near me and feel her strong love surround me. I never feel alone. When making long trips by car on the turnpike, I believe that she is next to me watching the road for me, just as she did while in this life and body. And, there are occasions, especially at night when I am quiet, that I swear that I feel a nudge. Sometimes in the night or early morning, I feel that her presence is next to me, and I almost reach out to her or turn to speak to her. Whenever I attend a major event by our children and grandchildren, I feel her presence and affirming love around us. I am confident that she watches our children and our two grandchildren who are very talented in religious, classical, and serious music and in drama at church events, at operettas, and at school.

Many months later, I now call her name and talk with her all day long. I involve her in all of my activities and tell her how much I love and miss her. I have pictures of her on my kitchen table and in most rooms of the house. I include her in family events with children and grandchildren, in my cooking, in my eating, in my hospital visitation, and in my church events.

During this period, I have also come to a renewed relationship with my mother and my father, who had died in 1986 and in 1997. I am forever and totally grateful for the upbringing that they gave me. They gave me a strong and healthy body, and helped me develop a strong mind. They each taught me integrity, dedication, hard work, a conservative intellectual life, the classics, the reality of the unseen, and most importantly to accept our creator as the sustainer of all life. My father taught me to think in theological terms about my faith. My mother passed to me an appreciation for the finest music. They are in large measure responsible for whom I have become. I have always felt close to each of them throughout their lives, and sometimes many years ago, during the day while separated by the miles, I used to feel mutual understanding and closeness while my mind imagined what they were doing.

Calvin Keeler, Sr.

Unfortunately, there was one choice that I made with which they did not agree at all, and they certainly let me know that. Occasionally as I matured, I would use my best "management" skills to try to effect a change in them. Sometimes I succeeded and sometimes I failed, but I always maintained a sincere appreciation for what they had done for me. Once after a difficult discussion of issues, I stated that we were family and that we needed to work together in this issue, and that we would be together and close forever. Today, I have the distinct feeling that they now fully understand my decisions. I never broke the bonds of our relationship and am privileged to respect and to belong to each of them. However, I now feel that there is a much deeper understanding of who I am and a more complete acceptance of each for the other.

I believe that there are several factors about Jane that enabled her to survive so many surgeries and so much sickness, and to be able to exceed the best medical advice about her life expectancy by forty-five years. These are the factors that promoted her healthy lifestyle.

- She had a vibrant faith in God and a strong prayer life, and knew that she belonged to Him.

- She knew real love in the life that we shared together, and was surrounded by the love of her family. Before our son, Calvin, Jr., left for graduate school in 1976, the three of us were inseparable and had a true bond, never broken for even a moment.

- Until the last years of her life, she had a good diet of vegetables, meat, fish, and eggs.

- Until the last six years of her life she had plenty of exercise, in cleaning her house, in swimming, in boating, and in hiking in the hills and mountains

- She had minimal anxiety, even over her sickness, and had very few days of negative vibrations and conflict. She was always positive and happy, and always pictured herself as where she expected to be: well and happy.

It would be impossible to overstate her devotion for and her love for me throughout our entire relationship and marriage. No one ever received so much love and care as I have received. She seemed to come by it so naturally—it was just her way. I often ponder why I was so fortunate. For my part, I also felt total devotion and love for the most important person in my life. I can honestly say that neither one of us was ever attracted to anyone else.

I believe that we were put together to help each other, to grow together, to support each other, and to learn many of the lessons of life together. It was not a random choice, but placed there by the Almighty for us to accept or reject by our own free will.

I have been overwhelmed by the enormity of the decisions that we made along the way so that we could find each other and spend our lives together. With my spiritual faith and the love of my wife, I need or desire nothing else from this world. I feel uniquely blessed.

Calvin Keeler, Sr.

Since the death of my wife, I have remained active and cherish all of the greatest memories any man could have. Our son and daughter-in-law and two grandsons have been outstanding to me. Jane was correct that I needed to be with our family after she was gone. I have also made many visits to the extended family in Connecticut and in Virginia. I have become very active in church work and have become the Minister of Visitation, which enables me to visit those who are sick in the hospital and in the health care units of nursing homes. Since I attend a large and active church, I have many to see, and I keep very busy. My special ministry is to the terminally ill and then to assist with their funeral services. This must be something that I am supposed to do, since in the last two years, the number of terminally ill people with whom I have visited and prayed has astonished me.

I still have the great gift of life. Rather than being overwhelmed and stymied by the question, what do I do now? I have decided to make a difference wherever I can and to use my wonderful experiences to share my love and my faith with others.

I truly look for that day when I will be in the presence of my creator and when I shall be able to hear my wife once again, and also my father and my mother, as they all hear and see me now. It is my expectation that I will be welcomed into a more glorious life, in the presence of God, and surrounded by loved ones. What a great day that will be! I will celebrate the completion of this journey and my lessons, and the start of a new life, triumphant and eternal. Of what should I be afraid? Until then, I shall do my best to share this experience and my faith with others about me, and wish that everyone could have as great a life and family as I have had.

Calvin Keeler, Sr.

Chapter 11

The Lessons of Life

Jane and I believed that we were placed here in this life to learn how to live and to learn about God and his love. Learning how to live well is more difficult than is commonly understood, and we knew that we would need to learn many lessons, so that we would be able to contribute to the world around us and to share in eternal life with our creator. Many lessons came from scriptures, but some of Jane's lessons came from her education, from her experiences, from her living, and from her vision and intuition of the next life.

It is up to us and our own decisions as to how well we learn those lessons and how well we live. We believed that in the next life we will account for our progress or lack thereof. In her lifetime, Jane demonstrated that she had learned many of her lessons. However, neither Jane nor I ever believed that we had learned all of our lessons, or that we had learned them perfectly, for we are only human. I confess that I am still learning. Each of us has our own, often unique, lessons to learn, and following are some of ours, that we humbly suggest. The lessons that life offers to each person to learn will surely be different, and it will require discipline, dedication, and meditation for one's whole life to discern one's own lessons. It is truly a life-long endeavor for each of us.

The Great Commandment is the most basic lesson to be learned and to incorporate into one's life. "Love the Lord your God with all your heart and with all your soul and with all your mind. This is the first and greatest commandment. And the second is like it: Love your neighbor as yourself." (Matt 22:37–39)

For the both of us, our ability to survive and even thrive for this extended period of illness resulted directly from our early faith and grounding in a commitment to God. We believe that he nurtures us, supports us, loves us, and is always with us, for we were and are never alone. Because of our human limitations and frailties, it is the power of God in our lives and not our own abilities that enables us to become who we are. It is God who gave us His guidance, who taught us what is important in life, and who taught us how to live. From Him we learned right from wrong, and we learned about sacrificial love.

We worked on developing our faith for all of our lives. There is nothing more important than committing our lives to our faith in and to our aware-

Calvin Keeler, Sr.

ness of the power of God, even though we cannot see Him or rationally prove His existence. Without being God-centered, we believed that we could never reach the fullness of our potential. This dedication to the maturing of our faith began while we were yet toddlers and lasted throughout our entire lives. If there is inadequate dedication of ourselves while still a child, or "time off" from this journey of maturing our faith, even in the adventures and excesses of teenage youth and early adulthood, then there will be gaps and some truths that we may never learn. "Time off" means an excessive focus on this world and its objectives, and always a diminution of our ability to understand God. As frail human beings, we recognized our need for God, and we understood that we needed to learn humility and to contain human arrogance. Except for her pride in her family, I never once saw Jane proud or arrogant.

When it does come our time to die, we should not fear nor struggle in vain to prevent it, but allow ourselves to pass easily in trust and faith from this life to the next. Our souls will know when it is time, and our bodies need to release our souls at that point. We need to permit the Good Shepherd Jesus to carry us home. Sometimes it may be sudden or catastrophic, as with a major heart attack or a life-threatening injury, and there are no choices. When one dies, it will be all right. It is natural, and the cycle of life is a part of God's plan of creation and growth. Death is the separation of the soul or the spirit from the physical body, the joyous completion of our tasks here, and the entry into life triumphant and eternal. The soul does not die, rather this is how it is released for eternal life. Fortunately for us, however, while in this world the body is designed to struggle to remain alive and to work through sickness and pain and other impediments for as long as possible. Life is a very precious gift, and not a minute should be wasted. When all is totally lost, when the body's organs are failing fast, and when there is no hope here in this life, then Christ is our hope, and we should permit ourselves to look forward to the next life with joy and anticipation.

Throughout Jane's entire life, her doctors repeatedly told her that she was too sick to survive. At seventy years old, even up to the last hours of her life, she still expected another miracle: to get well and to return home. The miracle that she did receive was far grander than any of the miracles that she had previously received or anticipated.

On a related topic, I urge everyone to be kind and prayerful to those whom you may visit when they are in a final coma, for the soul of the coma-tose person understands and knows what is being said and done, even though the body may not be aware. In many cases of near-death experiences, it is reported that after the cessation of life here on earth, the individual at first rises slightly, sees himself or herself from above, understands what is transpiring, and then sees a great light. At that point, the departed becomes much less interested in the problems and issues of this life, including the manner of death, but

Calvin Keeler, Sr.

will instead focus on the true relationships of love in this world and in the next, and feel an overwhelming sense of love, peace, and happiness. We will then know that it is not just all right, but is very right. We should then follow that great light to the presence of God, where we may confess about the growth we have made in our life.

We firmly believe that Jesus will come to take us home and will be there to assist us in the process of crossing and judgment. We believe that it will then be determined whether or not we have learned the lessons of this life, and how we might progress further in God's presence. I also believe that God allows our loved ones who have already passed to be around us in this world, to watch over us, and to greet us in our passing. They love us, and wish to know that we still love and miss them. Some people use the words "angels" and "guides," but those words refer to other energies that God sends to help us.

We learned that through faith that our lives and souls had been redeemed, and that our humanness, our weakness, and our sinfulness had been overcome by God's grace. An unshakable faith is not determined by perfection, or by any number of creeds or "truths" but rather by a change in our lives and our own commitment to and acceptance of God as the foundation for our lives and the acceptance of his redemptive power. It is not possible to find redemption through obeying the law nor through good works, but rather through God's grace of being born again. It does not need to be a requirement for everyone to duplicate exactly how we lived, but we were both extremely active in church work, when able. We believed that the church does provide guidance as to the meaning of life and the nature of God.

Love comes from God, and He bestows it upon us all, sacrificially and unconditionally. We needed to accept that love and then witness it to all whom we met and knew. We needed to learn to reciprocate that love to our creator, to learn to love our close family, to learn to love all in our extended family, and to learn to be kind to and to love all with whom we came in contact. We should work to reconcile ourselves with all the members of our families and as many others as we can, and to adopt a gentler lifestyle. We believed that we each needed to learn one very difficult lesson: to never hold a grudge and to forgive anyone and everyone who had ever injured or insulted or snubbed us (Eph. 4:31–32). The lesson to forgive anyone who has ever wronged one is a very difficult lesson, and one that was difficult for Jane and took a lot of effort for her to learn. We needed to learn to reach out to others and always smile. Wherever and with whomever we can, we should always demonstrate kindness, gentleness, peace, and love.

One of the most important lessons is that each minute of life is a precious and valuable gift and is not to be wasted, for all of life is given to us by God! We both learned to enjoy this great gift. As finite human beings, we cannot create life, nor can we add an inch to our stature nor add a hair to our heads.

When life has been terminated, which we, as human beings, have the power to actually cause, we cannot ourselves restart life nor overcome death. It is over in a very final sense. God has granted us tasks to do and lessons to learn in this life, and we believe that we should use all of our efforts to accomplish those tasks right up to the last minute, all while enjoying this marvelous and bountiful world around us. If we are here to learn our lessons and to teach others, then we must utilize every minute at all times in our lives, even near the end. Failure to utilize every precious moment will certainly result in achieving less in this life than what could have been possible.

Jane endured and survived, while receiving a maximum amount of modern acute-level medical attention, and yet felt with real thankfulness that each day of life was worth living, because it is better than not living, right up until there was no energy left in her body to support her spirit. She passed quietly and without fear, for she knew where she was going and why, and had filled her life with positive actions and thoughts about her God and her family.

She believed that we are all born with free will, and that we have the choice for good or for evil, for taking action one way or another. She believed that we always have a choice about the future, that nothing is so cast that it cannot be changed or modified. Further, we always have the choice of our reactions to whatever something or someone causes to happen to us. We must learn how to use that freedom of choice.

Too frequently, the path seems gray and the choices unclear. God will not force us along any one path or to make any particular choice, although at times, we may and should feel led. Using prayer and meditation, we must follow His guidance, when we believe that it is God who is leading us and when we can discern it. She knew that she had choices that were hers to make, and she also knew that there were times when she could discern God's guidance. All around us, we find evil, and there will be choices available that will not lead us in the best direction. God's gift of free will and our proper use of that are the only way to learn our lessons and to develop into true beings that can share in His creation.

Early in life, we are faced with some terribly large choices and decisions that will have a major impact on the entire future direction of our lives. We have the opportunity to learn to work as hard as we can and to study as much as we can. She believed that no effort should be spared at formal education, continuing discipline, and self-education for as long as we have breath. We are never too old. The more enlightened we can become, the more meaning life will have for us, and the grander the next life will be. She believed that we should enjoy hard work and discipline, and study the classics, literature, music, philosophy, psychology, as well as science. May we become the best that we can be and as smart as we can. Become as mature and self reliant as possible, always knowing that we are what we are by the grace of God and the freedom that He has given us to pursue this life as we choose. If one were to select happiness or pleasure as a goal, then there may be short-term good times which will fade away, but these are the wrong goals to adopt to learn one's lessons and to fulfill one's destiny.

Another lesson is the opportunity to develop a life of prayer, in which we first worship and praise God, and then ask for His help and guidance. She learned that prayer was a vital part of her life and her ability to overcome her illnesses. It was a part of her life from early childhood until her last day. We were fortunate that we each learned to pray on our knees. There is no requirement to fill each moment of prayer with talk, music, or activity (even church activity), but rather in quietness, waiting for God and asking Him to fill our lives with His power, His meaning, His guidance, and to protect us with His divine love.

We should meditate and wait for His inspiration, as Jesus did in the wilderness while being tempted, when on the mountaintop, and when in the garden, where he said, "Yet not my will, but yours be done" (Luke 22:42). Sometimes the answer may come as intuition or a strong feeling about what we should do. It will take all of our efforts and a preponderance of the evidence to differentiate true guidance from subjective feelings. We need to ask God to lead and direct our path. The phrase "in a still small voice" is very appropriate, since we cannot usually hear a voice, but we should consider that God might speak in the silence. Prayer and meditation can be done quickly when we are surrounded by a crisis or evil, or it can be in total quietness for as long as necessary. It is clear from the scriptures that Jesus found that solitude was His way.

Jane learned to develop bravery and courage, as we will all need these qualities when beset by problems later in life. Jane lived through times of extreme pain and discomfort in the hospital and at home, yet she never lost her courage or her vision. She suffered many very painful procedures over the years. She knew that God was close and always expected to get better to enjoy this life one more time. She fixed her vision on the eternal rather than on the pain of this world.

God's faithfulness radiated through her and touched many of those with whom she came in contact. The doctors and medical staff routinely commented on her faith, courage, strength, and desire to get well, and her wish to return to her home and to me. It is human and natural that as each new problem appears, it gets a little harder to face the future. We are reminded of that great poem "Footsteps." In the poem, the anonymous author wrote that in looking at the scenes of his life in his dream, he noticed times when there was only one set of footsteps in the sands of time. We remember that the Lord answered, "It was then that I carried you."

Jane taught us to never give up, and that every worthwhile endeavor that is important to us should be pursued with all the energy that we have, just as perfectly as we can. As she did, try to make each day

                                   Calvin Keeler, Sr.

normal and filled with constructive activities, without fear, anger, remorse, selfishness, or self-pity. On the other hand, it is very sensible and necessary to make an appropriate allotment of time for one's self, for vacation, relaxation and pleasure.

Jane and I studied and discussed how life-long relationships should be constructed very early in our dating. We came to believe that most people usually underestimate the importance of selecting the correct partner for marriage, due to infatuation or for fear of being left out. Due to our search of the scriptures and the ancient philosophers, we learned that it is important that the selection be based upon the compatibility of souls and life vision, rather than upon physical attributes or a search for happiness itself. Happiness is found not by seeking it, as most do, but by building a relationship based upon mutual trust and admiration. We urge each to try to find the other half to one's soul. This decision will have a profound impact on one's ability to grow and to develop for the rest of life, and also on any children that may come. We believed that it is important not to select the least bad of several bad choices or to have blind hope that the other partner will change.

With the correct marriage partner, one can establish a home of love, peace, and nurturing growth for the remainder of his or her life. As we matured, we learned that the goal should be total devotion and love for each other, and it should never be fifty-fifty, for a true marriage knows no limits and no bounds. Fifty-fifty often results in a lack of commitment and disappointments, as when one partner refuses to go beyond a certain point. Jane and I enjoyed the lifetime goal of total devotion to each other without limits or boundaries—one hundred percent. It should be understood that being human kept us from perfection. For the most part, there was no task or request that was unwelcome. It was a privilege that I could spend so much time with her during her last years in the hospital. She was never alone in the hospital in the dark of night.

We were an example of two people who were able to live separate lives with individual goals and career objectives, and yet who shared so deeply that it was as if we shared one consciousness. Our closeness for our entire life together was a source of comfort and support for each other, as well as being a witness for others to admire and to emulate. Many have told me about how much they admired us and wished they could find the same kind of relationship. Other than holding hands and little hugs, we were never outwardly demonstrative in public. Yet, everyone knew that we shared a deep love and were surrounded by happiness and peace. We wished that everyone would learn to remain true and committed to his or her partner and to reject all physical relationships outside of the bonds of marriage.

We were always thankful for the joy and the lives that we shared. We have always been there for each other, and at all times of stress with tenderness. If, before marriage, one questions whether his or her own selection for a partner could make that level

                    Calvin Keeler, Sr.

of commitment, then one probably needs to make another selection. We were thankful for the wonderful opportunity we had to share together in the rich abundant life that God has bestowed upon each of us. He has supplied meaning and purpose to each day.

Jane seemed to learn naturally to take care of her body, for it is where the spirit dwells while in this life, and it grants us the ability to be a meaningful part of this world. The body is more complex than we can yet understand, and life is a miraculous and precious gift, freely given. She learned to sustain her body with true love, clean air, exercise, adequate sleep, and good food (today we know that that includes minimizing such items as refined sugar, white flour, toxic chemicals, and packaged and fast foods). We also need to learn to control stress and thus limit its effects. I am convinced that Jane added decades to her lifetime by making these lifestyle choices of adequate exercise, good sleep habits, freedom from stress, and wholesome food with natural vegetables and fruits.

If our body becomes injured or damaged, there is no replacement, and we will certainly live with the results and a shortened time to enjoy this world. Fortunately for us, the body has marvelous curative and recovery systems that can work wonders in many cases of disease and injury. Whenever our body malfunctions, whether due to congenital defects, injury, infection, or inadequate respect, then we need to assist its restorative functions and to search for help through lifestyle changes, prayer and meditation, modern medicine, and other remedies of nature. If one gets gravely sick, then never give up and enjoy each moment that is left and each day to its fullest as much as possible. Along with medical support, Jane's care for her body gave it the strength to overcome many diseases throughout her life.

Together we learned not to let all of the illnesses overwhelm and change our lives or to keep us from normal and happy lives, even as we needed to accept the resulting limitations. We decided that we should always take care of each other, that living was more important than just existing, and that we each never wanted to be apart nor did we ever leave each other alone. We went on vacations, ate good food, visited family, moved for employment opportunities, enjoyed church work, and did all of the other things that a family should do in daily living. She never acted like an invalid, and we each should make a major effort to never act like an invalid anymore than our bodies require. For each of the thirty or more major surgeries, she entered the operating room without fear or anxiety, trusting that God would take care of her, that she would be in His hands, and that the doctors and medical staff would do their best. Whatever might happen, she knew that God was with her, that she had already had a good life, and that the rest was in God's hands. A very important fact of recuperation is to always visualize getting well and going home and to fully resuming normal living with all activities. This act of positive goal setting is what she did,

   Calvin Keeler, Sr.

and she benefited from its profound healing and restorative properties.

In summary, there are many lessons that affect our attitudes and lifestyle. We urge each person to enjoy life, smile a lot, work hard, take vacations, eat well, and show relatives and friends that you love them. Do not waste time or your life. Take the effort to find the right partner for life, one with whose soul there is compatibility at least as regards vision and goals. And, always ask in prayer for God to walk beside you and to guide you.

Life is a precious gift, and we should use every precious minute. One goal that we had in life was to show the spirit that God has given to us and to witness to God's great love. The creator wants us to share in his love, and then to witness and teach that love to others, so that they too may learn to share in his love. This is how to make a difference in this life and how to help those around us. Jane made each day meaningful, never wishing one moment away. Even at her worst times, she did not waste or wish life away.

From the midst of misery, suffering, and sickness, the author of the book of Job in the Old Testament asked "Why?" He said that the answer depends upon an understanding of the revelation of the omnipotence of God and that God is wisdom, power, and love (Job 38–42:6). The existence of God is the answer to every question. There are times when our creator enables the unbelievable healing powers that already exist in our body, and there are other times when He intervenes directly. His very real miracles in our lives are countless and ongoing. Our highest choice is to participate in and to experience the love that comes directly from God and was revealed to us by Jesus the Christ. We should then share that love with our whole family, friends, and those with whom we come in contact.

Appendix A

Jane Wiley Keeler

Born February 19, 1932 in Calais, Maine
She departed from this life June 15, 2002

ORDER OF FUNERAL SERVICE

*A service of worship and thanksgiving to God
for her life and her witness*

Christ Is Our Hope

Jane's funeral was held on Wednesday June 19, 2002, at the Ebenezer United Methodist Church in Newark, Delaware. The service was well attended by family, church friends and some hospital personnel. Jane made the musical selections (she knew exactly what she wanted)—they were beautiful, and she approved the scriptural selections.

It was a most beautiful service. Since her selections spoke so strongly of her faith, I have listed them as follows:

Musical preludes:

- "Guide Me O Thou Great Jehovah" setting by Flor Peeters
- "O Sacred Head Now Wounded" setting by Johann Pachelbel
- "Day Is Dying in the West"
- "It Is Well With My Soul"
- "Great is Thy Faithfulness"
- "Joyful, Joyful, We Adore Thee" setting by Gerhard Krapf
- "Jesu Joy of Man's Desiring" by J. S. Bach

Congregational singing:

- "How Great Thou Art"
- "He Leadeth Me: O Blessed Thought"
- "Abide With Me"

Special Music

- "Pie Jesu" arranged by Andrew Lloyd Webber - Duet by Daughter-in-law, Sharon Keeler, and grandson, Timothy Keeler

Musical postludes:

- "Trumpet Tune" by Henry Purcell
- "Water Music Suite" (selected movements) by G. F. Handel

    Calvin Keeler, Sr.

Opening scriptural sentences:

- Romans 8:37–39
- Psalm 27:1
- Isaiah 63:9
- John 15:12–17

Scriptural readings:

- Psalm 139: 1–4, 7–12,14, 17–18, 23–24
- Psalm 19: 1–3, 7–14
- Genesis 1: 1–4, 7,11 20, 25–27, 31
- Isaiah 40: 1–11, 25–26, 28–31
- John 14: 6–7, 15–17, 27
- II Corinthians 4: 6–7
- I Corinthians 15: 20–22, 35–36,38,42–44, 49–50, 53–58

The minister Rev. Ray F. Graham conducted the service, with the assistance of Rev. Bill Dore. The organist was Kerry W. Dietz. Kerry W. Dietz read the words from the husband. The duet sung by Sharon and Timothy was most beautiful and appropriate.

Jane was buried in the cemetery adjacent to the church. The pallbearers consisted of our son, my brother in law (Frank Estey) and three nieces (Jennifer Fee, Sandra Messer and Christine Mcaskill - all daughters of my sister Ann). Jane was buried in a beautiful blue summer light dress with flowing scarf, and we placed her favorite stuffed animal in the casket with her. I had purchased the stuffed animal, designed as an ultra light lamb for newborns, for her from a hospital gift shop during her first long stay in a medical intensive care unit two years previously. She often held the stuffed animal when she was a patient under sedation in the intensive care units when I had to leave at night, and the nurses knew that, and made sure it was close to her. In the final two years of her life, she must have spent five months in intensive care units. I left her wedding ring on her hand, for that is where it belonged. The casket selected had relief images that were among Jane's favorites: "praying hands" and *la pieta.* The service was a marvelous testimony of worship and thanksgiving to God for her life, and a witness to her faithful service.

On the day following the funeral while I was visiting the graveside and praying and meditating, I felt a profound sense of peace and well-being come over me. I knew Jane was okay. On the next day while praying and meditating, I felt a deep sense that we both had done all that we could have done. From that day forward, I have continued to know that our special love has survived her crossing and that it will endure unimpeded by our different realms. She is now in the presence of God forever.

Appendix B

Husband's Words for Jane Wiley Keeler at Funeral Service - June 19, 2002, 11 A.M.

This is a service of worship of God, creator, almighty, and redeemer, a service of recognition of God's daily miracles in our lives and a service of thanksgiving for the life and witness of Jane.

I must begin by giving thanks to our creator for bringing Jane into my life and for making it possible for me to share her life. I have been blessed beyond any expectations.

We were very happily married for over forty-eight years. Never have I known someone with such tenacity to live the life that she was given to the fullest. How fortunate I have been, for she has made my life better and added a touch of grace. She made my life easier and tried to make every day a happy one. We had the best of lives and did almost everything that we wanted to do. Life is very precious and not to be wasted. Life is a gift from God—it is good. Her message to us is that life is to be lived as long as the body can sustain it, and is not to be discarded lightly or early.

I cannot tell you how many hundreds (or thousands) of lives Jane has touched with her faith, her smiles, and her courage. What a shining light she was for truth and for God! I cannot tell you how many people that we together have touched with our shared love and commitment to each other and to the truth from above that overrides and supports all of us. She has made a statement with her life. That is all any of us can do. Last Sunday Jane's death was announced in the Lexington United Methodist Church. Several worshippers stood and testified how Jane's courage, smiles, and faith had touched their lives and changed them.

Jane was very special. What made her so special was that everyone she touched was inspired to a greater faith and to try a little harder. And that is the way that she lived her own life right up to the end.

Jane spent her early years in Calais, Maine. She moved to Hartford and went to the church that I was attending in 1942. We did not date until 1948. At an early age, she memorized all the verses on the daily bible calendar. Upon being tested, she missed only one. As a young person (and the only one I know who has done this), she learned two words out of the dictionary every night. Upon graduation from High School, she wanted an education. Since she had to work, she attended college night school four nights per week from 5 PM until 10 PM. Her chosen fields of interest were literature and writing. Her illness kept her from producing as an adult in her fields, but she is one of the best-educated persons that I know. I valued her knowledge and understanding.

She has been very ill for all of her life since 1954, and remained in poor health her entire life. And, I have lived under the threat of this day for over forty-eight years. Yet it does not make it any easier,

Calvin Keeler, Sr.

only harder, for the closer we have become each year and each day. She has lived with severe pain almost every day since that time. Yet, she never ceased to use the energy and life force that she had. She was one of the strongest that I have known in faith, courage, bravery, and spirit. She was always proper, brave, and tenacious. She was strong and had great integrity. How did she live well and prosper with all those illnesses for all those years? Only God knows. For she always kept going. She has fought the battle all of her life, and she believed that her life and her death were in God's hands. Her faith in her creator God never wavered. Through it all Jane knew whose she was. She never ceased to commune with her creator through prayer. She has set high standards for us for spirit, for devotion, for faith, for zest for and for the love of life, and for integrity. In the last years, she struggled to get to church to worship and sing. She loved to sing and hear her Christian hymns. I believe that Jane was chosen by God to live this example for life. I also very emphatically believe that we were chosen by God to be together. The last few days were especially hard as I watched her fade away, with all of her energy used up.

I shall miss her every minute of every day for the rest of my life. I shall remember her as strong, often stronger than I, walking straight, doing her daily life. However, as she wore out her body, her eyes, her ears, her lungs, her stomach and all of her physical strength, her spirit and faith actually grew as her body failed. We were equals, neither one was subordinate. She taught me much about faith, love, hard work, and living. Almost every evening she would stand in the window and watch for my car to turn into the driveway from work. And, especially she would watch on the stormy, snowy blizzard conditions that we had for so many years in New England. And, there was always a hot home-cooked meal ready to serve.

Her will was strong and her faith was strong. In her church in Lexington, Massachusetts that she attended regularly for over 30 years, two ministers knew her as "Saint Jane." Hundreds of people in hospitals and churches have been touched and inspired by her courage, faith, and bravery. Some have told me that she was such a warm person. Respected doctors have told us that she changed them both personally and professionally. She counts as friends many, many people in the Boston area and in the Lexington United Methodist Church. By her life, Jane was one who made a difference. She has set a standard, which is very very high for us. Fortunately, she has inspired us with her courage.

She felt very pleased to be loved by two churches in recent years. She was very pleased with her membership and connection to the Ebenezer United Methodist Church and how this church took her in, visited her, prayed for her, and enfolded her in love. In addition, she was pleased to continue her friendships, established over many years, with the Lexington United Methodist Church. They too kept her in their prayers and in their love each and every week.

The struggle for life is finished. She had the very best of the very best of medical care. And, she faced dozens of medical crises in her lifetime. She frequently had severe pain throughout her life, but the pain is gone, and the tears have been wiped away. She has been welcomed into the presence of God, and the Heavenly choir has sung. We may ask why, and why so much pain. But, there are no satisfactory answers to these questions in this world. There are **NO** answers. They are the wrong questions. The question should be, with her as an example, what are you and I going to do the rest of our lives with the life and energy that God has given to each of us. This is the message and question that we should always consider when we think about the limits of life. Life may not be fair as we see it, but God is good, and she and I each felt that each and every day. ***"What are you and I going to do with the life and energy that God has given to each of us?"***

She never faltered from trusting in God, for she knew he led her every step of the way. In her final days, I would hear her praying in her hospital bed by the hour. And in looking back at her life at the footprints in the sand, there were indeed times when there was only one set of footprints, when the Lord carried her gently and lovingly through the sicknesses and trials that she faced so many times.

She won the battle of life. She is not here anymore. She has moved triumphantly and gloriously into the presence of the Almighty, and she is entering upon a new and grander journey with her God.

The body gave out, but her spirit will always remain. Our bodies are given just so much energy (and it is different for each of us). We will never understand sickness and death in this life. Those are mysteries that we must take on faith.

As she and I have discussed many times, we now have to see through a glass darkly, and know only in part, but then we shall see face to face. We cannot understand the mysteries of life and death. We who lived with her and were associated with her have more that a memory in our hearts. I have her spirit, her contributions, and her faith wrought into the fabric of my existence. These are strong elements in my life. Thus, she is as present as the consciousness of ourselves is present. She and I put our lives in God's hands during our youth, He was always with us, we have never wavered or changed, and our lives will always be in His hands in this time and after.

In spite of all my theological training and Christian thinking, it was Jane who taught me about faith. It was simple, direct, and uncomplicated. She faced each and every surgery by just putting everything in God's hands. No need to worry, and whatever happened, was all right with her. It was God's will. She taught me how to work through pain and suffering. Pain was a constant companion. We talked about the book of Job. She agreed with Job: It is sufficient to know that God *IS* and that God is there with us in the midst of all of our problems. She accepted

Calvin Keeler, Sr.

pain and suffering and almost never asked, "Why me?" She did not feel sorry for herself, but was more concerned with just living the rest of her life fully. The question was not why did God do this to me, but what am I going to do with the gift of life that I have. She had so much she always wanted to do. Even in the last month she said that her very limited and pain-filled life was better than no life at all.

As a child, maybe at the age of 5 or 6, she used to make her neighborhood friends attend "Sunday school" in a barn behind her house. For all of her life she never strayed from her reliance on and faith in God. She sang in church choirs for many years, and she was the president of a group of about forty church young adults. In our early years, we attended Sunday school and church services four times on Sunday and attended two more prayer meetings during the week. She was a member of several church committees.

She understood the secret of life. She had a relationship with God, and understood who she was. That was a key to her happiness. Life, she knew, was a gift from God, freely given each day. Corliss Lamont, an obscure philosopher, may have said it best, "The wise man looks at death with honesty, dignity, and calm, recognizing that the tragedy it brings is inherent in the great gift of life." Her faith would change that humanistic approach by adding the word "faith" to the phrase of "honesty, dignity, and calm."

She had one great-unfulfilled dream. She wanted to write poetry, but was not able to do that. Due to the many great illnesses, she never had the strength to do the work to fulfill the promise received in her college years of praise for her written poetry.

She had the will to live, and the power to overcome a great deal. She worked very hard with dedication at her tasks. She was always very active and loved to take care of her house, cleaning every day and cooking for her family every meal. She loved to wait and watch for her family to come home, with the supper meal ready to be put on the table. She loved planning and going on vacations for the whole family. She included beaching and boating as active recreational activities. She had the life force, and life is good!

We were married on September 11, 1953. Looking back from the perspective of time, it is clear that this marriage was not an accident but that the hand of God was present.

She taught me about love, total and complete without condition or compromise. We made a witness to an honest and loving relationship throughout our lives. When we were dating, we talked about one of Plato's philosophical writings. Plato believed that sometimes two people meet and join together who are true half souls, making a whole soul together. This was the best relationship. We were known for walking hand and hand in airports, church, stores, and everywhere. A former ministerial friend gave her a book of "Hugs." Neither she nor I ever put ourselves first, but always tried to do things that would make the other happy. Marriage is not fifty-fifty, but total giving without reserve. We did not each have

Calvin Keeler, Sr.

our own space, but we shared space together. Each day she tried to make my life a better one. We fully understood the love embodied in the words, "in sickness and in health." Of course, as with every one else, we had our disagreements. But, they were of no real consequence to our relationship.

This is more than today's saying of "soul mates," a much deeper connection. Maybe, we shared souls. We had a telepathic link, and I heard her from a great distance of thousands of miles when she was frightened or had foreboding. At least twice, she woke me out of a sleep when we were miles apart when she was frightened. I heard her when she was worried. We joined in goals, hopes, aspirations, faith, philosophy, and theology first. Then we married. The modern practice of physical relations first provides the wrong basis for love and marriage, so it is no wonder that love in marriage is almost absent in modern culture. We shared true deep feelings of unspoken thoughts and feelings and joys. I have never seen two who had such deep, constant and true love. We had a wonderful life together: very rich in every way. Our love will endure forever. I was struck by her intelligence and grand style. What I lacked in the area of common sense, she more than made up and in my deficiency taught me. To me she was always very special, very beautiful, and statuesque. She had culture and bearing and was very comfortable and at home in the best of Boston's financial district classy parties and meetings.

As a mother, she had the knack and understood the psychology to open our son's eyes at a very tender age to God and all the wonders and mysteries of life. She introduced him in his early years to language, music, and literature. I give her great credit for his growth and maturing in his formative years.

It has been very difficult to watch her deteriorating condition these last few months. Even in these last difficult days of declining health and many problems, she and I enjoyed each day together, and counted each one a blessing direct from God. We said the days were precious. She was always marvelous to be near. Since her most recent diagnosis in the year 2000, we both felt that the days we shared and the delays in the final stages of her disease were truly a miracle. They were not supposed to be.

She loved her whole family, and especially her son, her daughter in law, and two grandchildren. Each of them brought joy and lightened the load for her. She was very proud of each and of their accomplishments.

She believed that there were no endings in life, just changes, new opportunities, and new discoveries.

Perfection does not occur anywhere in this life. You may think that these comments are too biased and not accurate, but this is the impact that she has made on me and the memories that I shall always cherish, and I make no apologies for my statements. I have been blessed beyond words every day. My life is rich with love and family. I thank God every day and every hour for the blessings that he has bestowed

                                    Calvin Keeler, Sr.

on me. She and I had something very special. She was the most wonderful person I have ever known.

I have some final thoughts about the grace and providence of God for us. As did Jane, treat each day as a sacred gift from God to do with as much as you may. It is up to our free choice and us as to what we do with it. I recently heard something worth repeating: "We all are born and we all die; it is what we do in between that matters." Remember that God loves you, and that He has a plan for you. Just fill each day with true meaning. I pray that you may experience gentleness and not anger or strife, I pray that you will not be a user, I pray that you will forgive and find forgiveness, I pray that you will accept and be accepted, that you will reconcile and be reconciled, and that you may love and be loved.

As a final suggestion, I urge that you let the spiritual life of Christ within you grow and that you let God take control of your whole life: spiritual, physical and material, for Christ is our hope. Take the time and the effort to understand life and from whence it comes. The life of the spirit can be rich beyond words. My wife has left her imprint on me and on each of us here today for the rest of our lives. It is our choice what we will do.

I shall never forget holding hands, our sitting together in church, our walks through the woods, our quiet sails on the ocean on calm days, our standing on sandy beaches, the bustle of washing and cleaning and the wonderful odors and tastes of her superb cooking. I remember when she and our son planted a large garden of flowers, which the rabbits then ate overnight. I remember her keeping two ovens and four burners going with cooking continuously. I remember her loving cleaning and dusting!!! I remember our son taking his mother racing one Sunday in his daysailor. Upon returning, she exclaimed about passing other boats, and of seeing "cats paws" on the calm ocean top from gentle breezes. I remember her task when returning to the harbor in our larger boat of going forward and standing in the bow, waiting and then picking up the mooring and attaching it. Or, the time when we were first learning to sail, and we accidentally dropped a beach pail overboard. We decide to try a man overboard drill. We turned the boat around and approached the pail. It sank beneath the waves, and our son said, "Well, there goes mom." I remember the anniversary when I bought her a very big lobster at a fine restaurant and her eating and enjoying every bite as I cracked it open for her. Thank you for all the years of love and companionship, and I shall miss you terribly. I have been blessed with a wonderful partner and companion for my whole life. I am certain that God's plan will bring us together again the near future.

I thank God for allowing us to share our lives, and for being with us every day of our lives. These last several years have been very, very precious indeed. And Jane, I thank you for walking beside me and for sharing your life with me. We had something very special, not experienced by very many. You did

Calvin Keeler, Sr.

more than just share your love with me. We will not be apart for long.

I have one more thing to say. I pray that each one of you may know for himself or herself the joy of that type of shared love, where there is no 50–50 and where you can share a life and share experiences. Share your thoughts, your dreams, and your aspirations. Further, on a different note if I will be permitted to continue, in the next life I believe that we will be surrounded by God's love and truth, and that we will re-experience our lives from the perspective of ourselves, from the perspective of those with whom we were involved and from the perspective of eternal truth, which will strip away our lies and self justifications and rationalizations. We are all human and all are failures. God will let us know that it is not right to hurt others, but if we are sincere, we will be forgiven and accepted into His love. Love each other and share each other's life. Be kind to those with whom you meet. Be aware of the pain you might cause someone else. Those who adhere to harshness, violence, selfishness, or hatred will naturally select themselves for a place without love and kindness. What is important in this life is how we live and how we touch others.

I will close with some words from a very important doctor at the Massachusetts General Hospital. "Words are hard to find adequate to this loss for you and your family. Being witness to Jane's courage, and to your love for and dedication to each other, has been one of the defining experiences of my life, professional or otherwise."

Learning from Jane

Thank you Jane. You were one of God's very special children - a miracle. I know that I am prejudiced, but I believe we lost a very special person from this world. May God hold you lovingly in the palm of His Almighty hand for all eternity.

Calvin Keeler, Sr.

Appendix C

*Words of Condolence Received
by Email and by Card*

" . . . My thoughts, best wishes and affection are with you both. I think of you and Jane from time to time each day since our last conversation. . . . Words are hard to find adequate to this loss for you and your family. Being witness to Jane's courage, and to your love for and dedication to each other, has been one of the defining experiences of my life, professional or otherwise."

*Doctor at MGH
(Massachusetts General Hospital)*

" . . . May I extend my most sincere sympathy on Jane's death. It was a blessing that it was so peaceful. There is only one person who labored as long and as hard as you did on this illness—and that, of course, was Jane herself. From one point of view, she has won the victory (St. Paul), i.e. everlasting peace. My prayer is for Jane, you and your family. . . Requiescat in pace"

Doctor at MGH

"My best wishes to you and your family at the end of this long and arduous struggle. You have turned out to be a wonderful doctor. The relationship that you and Jane constructed over the years was truly a wonderful thing for others to see. I've certainly profited by the experience of knowing you both."

Doctor at MGH

"I was so sorry to hear about Jane. The two of you had such a special relationship, no amount of time would ever seem enough. But, you can know in your heart that you were by her side throughout all the good times and bad. I know how much that meant to her. I hope the better days and times hold the memories that you will take with you into the future."

Social Worker at MGH

"Thank you so much for sharing your eulogy of Aunt Jane with me. It is deeply moving and I must read it again and again. You invested yourself fully and gave great thought and care to this important message - - this is so evident. You have truly honored Aunt Jane and shed light on her life and on your life together.

"You know that every Sunday night, on our way to church, I would ask Papa [her name for my father] how Aunt Jane and you were, knowing that you regularly called Papa on Sunday afternoon. In this way you were both in all of our thoughts and part of our weekly journey to church. Papa loved you both, as you well know. It has been a source of comfort to me to know that Papa is now in the best and kindest of fatherly hands, and so now is Aunt Jane. They fought the good fight and that is all we are supposed to. At least so it seems to me."

Niece

                                    Calvin Keeler, Sr.

"I read the words that you shared at Jane's funeral. As always, you spoke with truth and love. It was truly a marvelous witness to Jane's faith and to the longevity of your relationship with each other and with God. I especially appreciated your pointing out how her faith grew as her body failed. I was a witness to this, myself. And I also like the challenge that you issued to everyone who was there - 'What are you and I going to do with the life and energy that God has given to each of us?' That is a significant question to ask daily - even as Jane did, despite all of her compromises. How blessed you were to meet the "other half" of your soul that made you whole."

Minister at Lexington Church

"Thank you for sharing with us what you wrote and read about Jane at her funeral on your recent visit to LUMC [Lexington United Methodist Church]. Both of us read it and, as we have said before, we were touched by your comments, your ideals, and your TOTAL commitment to Jane throughout her long illness. We have great admiration for the way you have lived your life through all of her long and courageous struggles."

Friends at Lexington Church

"I can visualize Jane sitting in the church in the '70's with porcelain white skin, reddish hair drawn back, and immaculately dressed - always the Lady."

Friend at Lexington Church

"She was a beautiful woman, and I'll never forget her."

VNA nurse

"I will always remember Jane's smile and sense of humor and I will always remember and admire your tenaciousness in getting what she needed"

Nurse at MGH

"Jane was such a strong person. She cast that image to everyone. You have been such a strong person and certainly a loving husband. You were always at her side. . . . My fondest memory will be seeing Jane welcoming the LUMC carolers into your house. Her smile was steadfast (and she never complained about our singing). I admired Jane's strength and her faith."

Friend at Lexington Church

"We are so thankful that we could come. . . . and participate in the service for Jane. It was truly meaningful, and I do think she would have been pleased. The service was 'not from the book', as you expressed it, but from the heart."

Cousin

"Jane's long and difficult struggle is finally over. We remember her as devout in her faith - an example for all of us who knew and loved her, to follow. Your love and constant care over the long years of Jane's

218Calvin Keeler, Sr.

suffering also provides us with a model of the perfect
marriage commitment."

Friend at Lexington Church

"Jane will always be my SAINT, and my model. I
treasure every moment I spent with her, and I have
wonderful memories! She certainly did her journey
well."

Very close friend in Lexington

"Jane was beautiful inside and outside, and your
devotion to her was a wonderful example to all of
us."

Friend at Lexington Church

"She lived with such grace and dignity through much
travail, even projecting warmth and humor seem-
ingly inconsistent with her suffering."

Relative

Appendix D

Excerpts From Delaware Physician's Letters

Jane was a patient at the Christiana hospital in Delaware from late December 2001, until her death on June 15, 2002, except for two short periods of a few days each during which she tried to recover at home. Her primary attending physician and internist, Stephanie Ciccarelli, M.D., wrote two letters during this period in order to assist the rest of the consulting physicians and the medical team with understanding her care at the hospital. I would like to recall excerpts from these two letters.

From a letter dated 6 January 2002–

"Despite Mrs. Keeler's prolonged poor functional physical status, she has maintained excellent cognitive function until the last several months. She has expressed to Mr. Keeler and to myself that she wished all medical treatments be continued as long as there was hope of her keeping her cognitive function. Mrs. Keeler has miraculously survived many events that many medical personnel would have considered futile and perhaps unethical. By no means is this the worst clinical status that Mrs. Keeler has faced.

" . . . Mr. Keeler reports that her cognitive function had significantly improved until the past eight or so days. Given her transient mental status improvements, Mr. Keeler feels that there is hope and

Calvin Keeler, Sr.

that honoring her wishes would be to continue with aggressive care. He also reports that Jane expressed that she is not afraid of dying. He is also faced with the dilemma of deciding on which side of the fine line we stand, honoring and treating her aggressively versus comfort care and ending her misery. He agrees that if mental status were not to improve . . . or other more devastating events were to occur, he would accept it as a more definitive sign that care and quality of life would be futile. We even discussed placing her on a morphine drip and providing only comfort care.

" . . . I have known this couple for 2 years, and accept their consistent wishes without much doubt. We have decided that if an imminent life-threatening event were to occur, a short attempt at resuscitation would be pursued; therefore, she will remain a full code at this time."

From a letter dated 28 May 2002–
" . . . I've known Mr. & Mrs. Keeler for 2 years. When I first met her, she was basically confined to a wheelchair and had significant medical problems and pain issues, but she had all of her wits about her. She has had great deterioration over the past 2 years. Even prior to her first admission to Christiana, she had suffered through a great deal and miraculously recovered from many deathbeds. In fact, in 1996, she was sent home with hospice after a 9-month hospitalization to die.

"If it were my decision, I completely disagree

with Mr. Keeler to continue to provide ventilation and dialysis. . . . It is Mrs. Keeler's decision, then Mr. Keeler's by proxy. . . . I have continued to respect them. . . . Mrs. Keeler has lived through many previously predicted deaths. Who are we to say that we know for 100% certain that there are no further miracles ahead? Mr. Keeler agrees that one day (and one day soon), another terrible insult will occur, and that Mrs. Keeler will die. However, with all the miracles she's had and her previously expressed wishes to live and continue getting very aggressive care (which I have witnessed), Mr. Keeler is unable to give the order to stop ventilation or dialysis."

    Calvin Keeler, Sr.

Appendix E

Several Of Jane's Favorite Recipes

Jane was a natural and gifted cook, who feared no recipe and would attempt almost anything. Her cooking was wonderful, and so I have included several of her favorites.

Famous Oatmeal Cookies

3/4 cup vegetable shortening or margarine
1 cup firmly packed brown sugar
1/2 cup granulated sugar
1 egg or egg white
1/4 cup water
1 teaspoon vanilla
3 cups Quaker Oats (quick or old fashioned, uncooked)
1 cup all purpose flour
1 teaspoon salt (optional)
1/2 teaspoon baking soda
Spices: Cinnamon, Allspice

Heat oven to 350 F. Beat together shortening, sugars, egg, water, and vanilla until creamy. Add combined remaining ingredients; mix well. Drop by rounded teaspoonfuls onto ungreased cookie sheet. Bake 12 to 15 minutes or until light golden brown. Cool 1 minute on cookie sheet; remove to wire cooling rack. Store in tightly covered container. (For variety, stir raisins, chocolate chips, chopped nuts or coconut into batter.)

Makes about five-dozen cookies.

Orange Cranberry Nut Bread

1 cup sugar
4 tablespoons butter
1 tablespoon grated orange rind
1 egg
1/2 cup orange juice
2 cups all purpose flour
1 1/2 teaspoons baking powder
1/2 teaspoon baking soda
1 teaspoon salt
1 1/4 cups fresh cranberries, coarsely chopped
3/4 cup walnuts, coarsely chopped

Cream butter and sugar, add orange peel and egg, and mix well. Stir in juice. Add the dry ingredients. Stir to moisten. Fold in berries and nuts. Pour into greased 9x5x3 loaf pan

Bake at 350 for 50 - 60 minutes.

Gelatin Salad

1 package lemon Jell-O
1 cup hot water
1 cup pineapple
1 tablespoon vinegar

Calvin Keeler, Sr.

dash salt

      Mix above ingredients and let set until it starts
to firm up. Whereupon add:
1 cup celery chopped
1 cup pineapple
1 cup shredded carrots
a few cherries for color
add a few walnuts

      Pour into greased mold and chill until firm.

Holiday Punch

      Serves about 20 people

4 quarts ginger ale
2 cans frozen grape juice (mixed)
2 cans frozen lemonade (mixed)
4 cups orange juice
2 quarts orange sherbet

      Combine first four ingredients. Spoon chunks
of sherbet to float on top a quart at a time.

Apple Fruit Cake

1/2 cup butter
2 cups apple pie filling (canned)
1 cup sugar
2 cups all purpose flour
2 teaspoons baking soda
1/2 teaspoon salt
2 teaspoons cinnamon

1 teaspoon cloves
1 teaspoon nutmeg
1 teaspoon allspice
2 cups raisins
2 cups currants
2 cups candied fruit
2 cups candied cherries (red and green)
1/2 cup citron
1/2 cup candied pineapple
2–3 cups of pecans

In a saucepan melt butter; add apple pie filling and sugar. Heat, stirring occasionally until sugar melts. Cool. Mix dry ingredients together and thoroughly mix with fruits and nuts. Combine the two mixtures and pour into a foil lined 9-inch tube pan.

Bake at 300 for about 2 hours. Serve with a hard sauce.

Brownies

3 1 ounce squares *semi-sweet* chocolate
1 1 ounce square unsweetened chocolate
1 cup butter
2 cups sugar
4 eggs
2 teaspoons vanilla
1 cup flour
2 cups walnuts

In large saucepan, melt chocolate squares and butter over low heat. Remove from heat; add

Calvin Keeler, Sr.

Contact Calvin Keeler, Sr.
calvin.keeler@worldnet.att.net

Or order more copies of this book at

TATE PUBLISHING, LLC

127 East Trade Center Terrace
Mustang, OK 73064

(888) 361 - 9473

Tate Publishing, LLC

www.tatepublishing.com